REASON AND EXISTENZ

REASON AND EXISTENZ

FIVE LECTURES
BY KARL JASPERS

translated with an introduction by
WILLIAM EARLE

FARRAR, STRAUS AND GIROUX
NEW YORK

Copyright © 1955 by the Noonday Press

Library of Congress catalog card number 55-8231

Nineteenth printing, 1978

SBN 374.5.0060.6

Manufactured in the U. S. A.

These lectures on reason and Existenz were held in the Spring of 1935 upon invitation from the University of Groningen, Holland, as public lectures. The first edition appeared with J. B. Wolters, Groningen, 1935. This third edition is unchanged.

The translation was made from the third edition, Johs. Storm Verlag, Bremen, 1949*

* *Notes by translator are included within square brackets.*

TABLE OF CONTENTS

FIRST LECTURE: Origin of the contemporary philosophic situation (the historical meaning of Kierkegaard and Nietzsche)   19

SECOND THROUGH FOURTH LECTURES: Basic ideas for the clarification of reason and Existenz:

   Second Lecture: The Encompassing   51

   Third Lecture: Truth as Communicability   77

   Fourth Lecture: Priority and limits of rational thinking   107

FIFTH LECTURE: Possibilities for contemporary philosophizing   127

NOTES   151

INTRODUCTION

The text, of course, speaks for itself. But it may be of some assistance to the reader coming to Jaspers for the first time in English to have in mind the basic intent of his philosophizing. And, first of all, this intent has little to do with setting forth a new hypothesis about anything. Jaspers is not interested in sketching a picture of the physical world, or in outlining the nature of man, or in giving us a new metaphysical theory. Rather his philosophizing is designed to *reawaken* us to our own authentic human situation. And this situation, he is convinced, is of such a sort than any effort to freeze it conceptually or dogmatically, any attempt to schematize it exhaustively, or turn it into something known, must end both in a falsification of the situation itself and in a destruction of our own authentic possibilities. It is the aim of his philosophizing, then, to call attention to the limits of knowledge, not with the sceptical purpose of disposing of knowledge altogether, but rather in order to let the truth which always lies just beyond those limits shine through for a moment. Jaspers' philosophizing lives on the limits, turned both to what lies within and to what lies without. It remains on these limits and does not pass into a new theory of what is in principle beyond theory. Philosophizing here is a movement of transcending; and it is a movement which each must enact for himself.

The name for what is at last beyond the relativity of all our perspectives, horizons, and conceptual schemes, is "the Encompassing," *das Umgreifende*. This name is nothing but an index, or signum. It is not a word with a fixed, knowable connotation. It denotes the ultimate Being which is the foundation for our concepts but which can never be exhaustively grasped by them. Such a term, like all the key terms in Jaspers' philosophizing, has a clear *use;* but it has no clear, distinct, objective content.

"The Encompassing" as it is used to designate the world seems rather easier to grasp than it does in its correlative usage where it designates man himself, a use prominent in these lectures. For, in Jaspers' view, not only is the world and Being itself an Encompassing, but *man himself is an Encompassing*. That is to say, man himself is always more than what he can know himself to be. In principle, he is never exhaustible by any conceptual or scientific knowledge. The theoretical identification of man with what man knows himself to be has the inner effect of destroying precisely that freedom and authenticity which is the essence of man. He loses himself in the picture he has formed of himself. It is a sense of this always impending loss which lends to Jaspers' thought its moral earnestness. Something more is at stake than opposed theories; in this case it is the nature of man which can either be fostered or corrupted by man's self-comprehension.

Jaspers treats man as analyzable on three levels. First he is simply an empirical existent, *Dasein*, something which lives in space and time, a thing among other things. Secondly, he is consciousness as such, *Bewusstsein überhaupt*, the abstract understanding by which he comprehends essential connections among eternal truths, as in mathematics. Finally, he is spirit, *Geist*, that aspect which strives to embrace all of his experience, life, and culture within certain ideal totalities. These three levels are called "modes" of that Encompassing which we are; for each is, on its own level, an infinite and inexhaustible dimension. So far, however, we have not touched upon the central point which each man most authentically is. This fundamental center, each individual in his inwardness, as he is to himself as just this unique, historical self, is *Existenz*. "Existenz," again, is an index; it names without characterizing. What it names is not the individual in his organic vitality, his abstract understanding, or his spirit; it is the individual himself, as he comprehends himself, in his freedom and authenticity standing before Transcendence. It is the ultimate ground, basis, or root of each historical self; it is not the content of any concept. And since Existenz is actual only in authentic self-awareness, a corruption of that awareness may corrupt Existenz itself. Existenz is but a possibility for men; it is not a property with which we are endowed by nature. It must be enacted inwardly if it is to be at all; and it need not ever be. It is the possibility in men of coming to themselves, of the self rejoining itself for a moment. Existenz is only a possibility for human nature; things in the world have no such possibility. This is not, of course, to deny that things exist, but rather to signalize that they exist in a way radically different from authentic human existence. It is for this reason that we have retained the German Existenz throughout in our translation; it may serve as a constant reminder that at these points Jaspers is not talking about existence as that term is customarily used in all modern languages.

Existenz is unique, historical, and, taken in itself, *isolating*. As such it tends to corrupt into something inauthentic, self-willed, defiant. It sinks back into empirical existence. But one act of Existenz is reason. Reason is taken by Jaspers in its most comprehensive sense: it is the *ratio* which binds together the diverse; it is the bond which can unite anything with its other. And fundamentally, it can unite diverse Existenzen; such a union, communion, or communication is truth. There will be as many senses of truth as there are levels in the communicating human beings. Thus Jaspers' analysis of truth rests upon a series of connected ideas: reason as a bond, binding as communication, and actual truth as a mode of historical communication.

Such are the principal themes of these lectures. The problem is the polarity (and not opposition) of reason and Existenz. Each has limits; and there is no theoretical resolution of the problem. There is nothing but the possibility of resolution in unique historical moments between authentic persons where reason is kept open and free for an encounter with what may be most alien to it. The truth which may arise in such encounters is not expressible in theory or teachable doctrine.

Jaspers' philosophy as a whole is Existenz-philosophy. That is to say, problems are considered only insofar as they touch Existenz. The world is not considered as something in itself, but as that in which Existenz is, and toward which Existenz may be oriented. This phase of his thought is called world orientation, *Weltorientierung*. His philosophy comes to a focus in the illumination or clarification of Existenz, *Existenzerhellung*. Here, as elsewhere, there is no search for explanation or causal theory; the clarification of Existenz lights up its possibilities, its relations to other Existenzen and to Transcendence; it is a clarification of Existenz to itself. Such a clarification ends in no "psychology"; the situation of Existenz, its possible emergence, its tension toward Transcendence and other Existenzen are not unambiguously stateable; in the end, they can only be enacted. A third phase of Jaspers' thought is the exploration of symbols used to designate Being, *Metaphysik*. And again we find there is no possibility of an adequate, literal description. There are only symbols which have the possibility of taking on ultimate significance for Existenz, but also retain their capabilities for misleading. They can only point; it is up to Existenz to see where they point.

All expressions in Existenz-philosophy are ambiguous *in principle*. All its essential terms may be taken not as the indicators which they are, but as literal descriptions. Its "propositions" may be taken as objective assertions about a knowable object. Such a misinterpretation is always possible and cannot be prevented by further words, by warnings and instructions; for they too can all be misinterpreted. But Existenz-philosophy may have the effect of needling the reader to perform the same inner acts of transcending which Jaspers intends. This is neither mysticism nor simple incommunicability; it is a recognition that only Existenz can understand Existenz. Thus, for Jaspers, the most essential thing men have to say to one another cannot quite be said; or rather, its comprehension cannot be forced, nor can its truth be objectively established. Nevertheless, it remains the most important thing, and it remains true. Such expressions are corrigible only in existential communication, by authentic Existenz. There is, as Jaspers insists, an *essential* risk in such matters.

Readers therefore who are habituated to certain strains of contemporary Anglo-American philosophy will certainly be irritated by what seems like a lack of definition in Jaspers' key terms. What is Existenz? What is the Encompassing? What is Transcendence? We are told the roles of these terms in his thought, but not what they mean in any testable fashion. But this feature of his thought is not accidental, nor is it to be ascribed to some stylistic flaw. It lies at the very heart of what he wishes to say. To give "definitions" of these terms would be to contradict the intent of his philosophy. Nor, for this reason, are they "meaningless"; their meaning arises only at the extreme limits of reason. They designate ultimately what is "other" to reason. Does reason have this power of touching its own limits for a moment and "feeling" that which lies beyond? Can it transcend itself? Jaspers insists it not only can but must if it is to remain honest and clear. The situation is as though we stood in a small pool of light encompassed by the vast darkness. Someone calls attention to the encompassing darkness; where is it, the others cry, turning their torches out to light up and see the darkness, but of course they see nothing but more and more illuminated areas. Nevertheless, can we not be aware of this darkness as the limits of our light? The eye cannot literally *see* the dark, but is it not aware of it? And, Jaspers would insist, we must be aware of that darkness if we are not to forget what light means. Our sciences become corrupt in their own line of clarity if they become absolute. And now, what if our small pool of light were itself darkness, and the encompassing darkness, the real light?

In one sense Jaspers' philosophizing gives us nothing; we leave it with no new image of the world, no recipes for a happy life. But if we have responded to it as Jaspers intends we should, we may emerge with something less tangible, less arguable, less teachable, but ultimately more revolutionary: a renewed sense of our own limits and of the encompassing mystery. There is neither pessimism nor optimism here; and there is nothing of Sartre, who sees man as a "futile passion." True, man ultimately comes to an awareness both of his limits and of what lies beyond by "shipwreck"; his reason, his Existenz, all must go down. But the shipwreck is not absolute; in and through the shipwreck something finally authentic appears for the first time. We cannot *will* our own destruction, nor does our destruction automatically lead to insight; it may however be the occasion for seeing something authentic and eternal which forever lies beyond. Nothing more can be said about such a Transcendence; it is not the proper subject matter for a new doctrine. Dogmatism is as out of the question here as anywhere else in Jaspers. Nevertheless, here is where human life has the opportunity of perceiving its ultimate unsayable meaning.

The intent of Jaspers' philosophizing then is simply to recall us to our authentic situation. This recall is not itself a doctrine; it is only the stimulus to an inward action each must perform for himself in communication with others. Jaspers' Existenz-philosophy is thus an attempt to consider and enact human honesty; it is philosophy, not as wisdom, but as the love of wisdom.

WILLIAM EARLE
Department of Philosophy
Northwestern University

REASON AND EXISTENZ

first lecture

THE ORIGIN OF THE CONTEMPORARY PHILOSOPHICAL SITUATION

The historical meaning of Kierkegaard and Nietzsche

I. HISTORICAL REFLECTIONS; THE CONTEMPORARY SITUATION.

The rational is not thinkable without its other, the non-rational, and it never appears in reality without it. The only question is, in what form the other appears, how it remains in spite of all, and how it is to be grasped.

It is appropriate for philosophizing to strive to absorb the non-rational and counter-rational, to form it through reason, to change it into a form of reason, indeed, finally to show it as identical with reason; all Being should become law and order.

But both the defiant will and honest mind turn against this. They recognize and assert the unconquerable non-rational.

For knowing, this non-rational is found in the opacity of the here and now; in matter, it is what is only enveloped but never consumed by rational form; it is in actual empirical existence which is just as it is and not otherwise, which is subsumed under just those regularities we experience and not others; it is in the contents of faith for religious revelation. All philosophizing which would like to dissolve Being into pure rationality retains in spite of itself the non-rational; this may be reduced to a residue of indifferent matter, some primordial fact, an impulse, or an accident.

The will utilizes these possibilities in knowledge to its own advantage. A battle arises for and against reason. Opposed to pure, transparent reason's drive toward rest within the conceivable, stands a drive to destroy reason, not only to indicate its limits, but to enslave it. We want to subordinate ourselves to an inconceivable supersensible, which however appears in the world through human utterances and makes demands. We wish to subordinate ourselves to the natural character of impulses and passions, to the immediacy of what is now present. These drives are now translated by the philosophy which adheres to them into a knowledge of the non-rational: philosophy expresses its falling into the non-rational, the counter-rational, and the super-rational as a knowledge about them. Yet, even in the most radical defiance of reason, there remains a minimum of rationality.

To show how the many-fold distinction between reason and non-reason appears at the bases of all thinking would require an analysis of the history of philosophy out of its own actual principles. Let us recall a few selected points.

To the Greeks this problem of Being was already present in myth. The clarity of the Greek gods was surrounded by the sublime incomprehensibility of Fate, limiting their knowledge and power.

Most of the philosophers touched incidentally, although in important ways, upon what was inaccessible to reason.

Socrates listened to the forbidding voice of the uncomprehended daimon. Plato recognized madness, which if pathological is less than reason, but if divinely begotten, more; only through madness can poets, lovers, and philosophers come to a vision of Being. To be sure, according to Aristotle, in human affairs, happiness was the result of rational deliberation, but not totally; happiness could appear without and even opposed to deliberation. For Aristotle, there were men, the *alogoi*, who had a better principle than deliberative reason; their affairs succeeded without and even counter to reason.

These examples stand alongside the general form of Greek thought, which opposed appearance to Being (Parmenides), the void to things (Democritus), non-being to genuine Being (Plato), and matter to form (Aristotle).

In Christianity, the opposition between reason and non-reason developed as struggle between reason and faith within each man; what was inaccessible to reason was no longer regarded simply as other than reason, but was a revelation of something higher. In the observations of the world, the non-rational was no longer mere chance, or blind chaos, or some astonishing principle surpassing reason, but was taken comprehensively as Providence. All the fundamental ideas of a rationally unintelligible faith could only be expressed in irrational antinomies. Every rational, literal interpretation of faith became a heresy.

In the succeeding centuries, on the other hand, Descartes and his followers attempted a radical grounding of reason upon itself alone—at least in the philosophical excogitation of Being which the individual accomplished by himself. Although Descartes left society, state, and church intact, the attitude of the Enlightenment arose as a consequence; with what I validly think and can empirically investigate, I can achieve the right organization of the world. Rational thought, in the sense of presuppositionless universality, is a sufficient basis for human life in general. From the beginning, however, a counter-movement worked against this philosophy of reason, whether it be called rationalism or empiricism. This counter-movement was led by men who, although in complete possession of rationality themselves, at the same time saw its limits: that other which was important before any reason, which made reason possible, and restrained it. Over against Descartes, stands Pascal; over against Descartes, Hobbes, and Grotius, stands Vico; over against Locke, Leibnitz, and Spinoza, stands Bayle.

The philosophy of the seventeenth and eighteenth centuries seems to work itself out in these great antitheses. But the thinkers were irreconcilable, and their ideas were mutually exclusive.

In contrast to this world of thought, the philosophers of German idealism made an astonishing attempt to create a reconciliation, seeing in reason more than reason itself. German philosophy in its great period went beyond all previous possibilities and developed a concept of reason which was historically independent. In Kant, a new beginning was created. This concept of reason got lost in the fantastic construction of Hegel but broke through again in Fichte and Schelling.

When one looks over the thought of centuries, the same thing always seems to happen: in whatever form this Other to reason appears, in the course of rational understanding it is either changed back into reason, or sometimes it is recognized as a limit in its place; but then in its consequences it is circumscribed and delimited by reason itself, or sometimes it is seen and developed as the source of a new and better reason.

It is as though at the bottom of this thought, even in all its unrest, there always lay the quiet of a reason which was never wholly and radically questioned. All awareness of Being grounded itself finally in reason or in God. All questioning was circumscribed by unquestioned assumptions; or else there were merely individual and historically inefficacious pioneers who never achieved a thorough understanding of themselves. The counter-movements against rationality were like a distant thunder announcing storms which could be released, but which were not yet.

Thus the great history of Western philosophy from

Parmenides and Heraclitus through Hegel can be seen as a thorough-going and completed unity. Its great forms are even today preserved in the tradition, and are rediscovered as the true salvation from the destruction of philosophy. For a century we have seen individual philosophers become objects of special studies, and have seen restorations of their doctrines. We know the totality of past teachings in the sense of "doctrines" perhaps better than any of the earlier great philosophers. But the consciousness of a change into mere knowing about doctrines and about history, of separation from life itself and from actually believed truth, has made us question the ultimate sense of this tradition, great as it is and despite all the satisfaction it has provided and provides today. We question whether the truth of philosophizing has been grasped or even if it can be grasped in this tradition.

Quietly, something enormous has happened in the reality of Western man: a destruction of all authority, a radical disillusionment in an overconfident reason, and a dissolution of bonds have made anything, absolutely anything, seem possible. Work with the old words can appear as a mere veil which hid the preparing powers of chaos from our anxious eyes. This work seemed to have no other power than that of a long continued deception. The passionate revivifying of these words and doctrines, though done with good intentions, appears as without real effect, an impotent call to hold fast. Philosophizing to be authentic must grow out of our new reality, and there take its stand.

II. KIERKEGAARD AND NIETZSCHE.

The contemporary philosophical situation is determined by the fact that two philosophers, Kierkegaard and Nietzsche, who did not count in their times and, for a long time, remained without influence in the history of philosophy, have continually grown in significance. Philosophers after Hegel have increasingly returned to face them, and they stand today unquestioned as the authentically great thinkers of their age. Both their influence and the opposition to them prove it. Why then can these philosophers no longer be ignored, in our time?

In the situation of philosophizing, as well as in the real life of men, Kierkegaard and Nietzsche appear as the expression of destinies, destinies which nobody noticed then, with the exception of some ephemeral and immediately forgotten presentiments, but which they themselves already comprehended.

As to what this destiny really is, the question remains open even today. It is not answered by any comparison of the two thinkers, but it is clarified and made more urgent.[a] This comparison is all the more important since there could have been no influence of one upon the other,[b] and because their very differences make their common features so much more impressive. Their affinity is so compelling, from the whole course of their lives down to the individual details of their thought, that their nature seems to have been elicited by the necessities of the spiritual situation of their times. With them a shock occurred to Western philosophizing whose final meaning can not yet be underestimated.

Common to both of them is a type of thought and humanity which was indissolubly connected with a moment of this epoch, and so understood by them. We shall, therefore, discuss their affinity: first, in their thought; second, in their actual thinking Existenz; and third, in the way in which they understood themselves.

A. What is common to their thought: the questioning of reason.

Their thinking created a new atmosphere. They passed beyond all of the limits then regarded as obvious. It is as if they no longer shrank back from anything in thought. Everything permanent was as if consumed in a dizzying suction: with Kierkegaard by an otherworldly Christianity which is like Nothingness and shows itself only in negation (the absurd, martyrdom) and in negative resolution; with Nietzsche, a vacuum out of which, with despairing violence, a new reality was to be born (the eternal return, and the corresponding dogmatics of Nietzsche).

Both questioned reason from the depths of Existenz. Never on such a high level of thought had there been such a thorough-going and radical opposition to mere reason. This questioning is never simply hostility to reason; rather both sought to appropriate limitlessly all modes of rationality. It was no philosophy of feeling, for both pushed unremittingly toward the concept for expression. It is certainly not dogmatic scepticism; rather their whole thought strove toward the genuine truth.

In a magnificent way, penetrating a whole life with the earnestness of philosophizing, they brought forth not some doctrines, not any basic position, not some picture of the world, but rather a new total intellectual attitude for men. This attitude was in the medium of infinite reflection, a reflection which is conscious of being unable to attain any real ground by itself. No single thing characterizes their nature; no fixed doctrine or requirement is to be drawn out of them as something independent and permanent.

1. SUSPICION OF SCIENTIFIC MEN

Out of the consciousness of their truth, both suspect truth in the naive form of scientific knowledge. They do not doubt the methodological correctness of scientific insight. But Kierkegaard was astonished at the learned professors; they live for the most part with science and die with the idea that it will continue, and would like to live longer that they might, in a line of direct progress, always understand more and more. They do not experience the maturity of that critical point where everything turns upside down, where one understands more and more that there is something which one cannot understand. Kierkegaard thought the most frightful way to live was to bewitch the whole world through one's discoveries and cleverness—to explain the whole of nature and not understand oneself. Nietzsche is inexhaustible in destructive analyses of types of scholars, who have no genuine sense of their own activity, who can not be themselves, and who, with their ultimately futile knowledge, aspire to grasp Being itself.

2. AGAINST THE SYSTEM

The questioning of every self-enclosed rationality which tries to make the whole truth communicable made both radical opponents of the "system," that is, the form which philosophy had had for centuries and which had achieved its final polish in German idealism. The system is for them a detour from reality and is, therefore, lies and deception. Kierkegaard granted that empirical existence could be a system for God, but never for an existing spirit; system corresponds with what is closed and settled, but existence is precisely the contrary. The philosopher of systems is, as a man, like someone who builds a castle, but lives next door in a shanty. Such a fantastical being does not himself live within what he thinks; but the thought of a man must be the house in which he lives or it will become perverted. The basic question of philosophy, what it itself is, and what science is, is posed in a new and unavoidable form. Nietzsche wanted to doubt better than Descartes, and saw in Hegel's miscarried attempt to make reason evolve nothing but Gothic heaven-storming. The will-to-system is for him a lack of honesty.

3. BEING AS INTERPRETATION

What authentic knowing is, was expressed by both in the same way. It is, for them, nothing but interpretation. They also understood their own thought as interpretation.

Interpretation, however, reaches no end. Existence, for Nietzsche, is capable of infinite interpretation. What has happened and what was done, is for Kierkegaard always capable of being understood in a new way. As it is interpreted anew, it becomes a new reality which yet is hidden; temporal life can therefore never be correctly understood by men; no man can absolutely penetrate through his own consciousness.

Both apply the image of interpretation to knowledge of Being, but in such a fashion that Being is as if deciphered in the interpretation of the interpretation. Nietzsche wanted to uncover the basic text, *homo natura*, from its overpaintings and read it in its reality. Kierkegaard gave his own writings no other meaning than that they should read again the original text of individual, human existential relations.

4. MASKS

With this basic idea is connected the fact that both, the most open and candid of thinkers, had a misleading aptitude for concealment and masks. For them masks necessarily belong to the truth. Indirect communication becomes for them the sole way of communicating genuine truth; indirect communication, as expression, is appropriate to the ambiguity of genuine truth in temporal existence, in which process it must be grasped through sources in every Existenz.

5. BEING ITSELF

Both, in their thinking, push toward that basis which would be Being itself in man. In opposition to the philosophy which from Parmenides through Descartes to Hegel said, Thought is Being, Kierkegaard asserted the proposition, as you believe, so are you: Faith is Being. Nietzsche saw the Will to Power. But Faith and Will to Power are mere *signa*, which do not directly connote what is meant but are themselves capable of endless explication.

6. HONESTY

With both there is a decisive drive toward honesty. This word for them both is the expression of the ultimate virtue to which they subject themselves. It remains for them the minimum of the absolute which is still possible although everything else becomes involved in a bewildering questioning. It becomes for them also the dizzying demand for a veracity which, however, brings even itself into question, and which is the opposite of that violence which would like to grasp the truth in a literal and barbaric certitude.

7. THEIR READERS

One can question whether in general anything is said in such thought. In fact, both Kierkegaard and Nietzsche were aware that the comprehension of their thought was not possible to the man who only thinks. It is important who it is that understands.

They turn to the individuals who must bring with them and bring forth from themselves what can only be said indirectly. The epigram of Lichtenberg applies to Kierkegaard, and he himself cites it: such works are like mirrors; if an ape peeks in, no apostle will look out. Nietzsche says one must have earned for oneself the distinction necessary to understand him. He held it impossible to teach the truth where the mode of thought is base. Both seek the reader who belongs to them.

B. Their thinking Existenz in its actual setting: the age.

Such thinking is grounded in the Existenz of Kierkegaard and Nietzsche insofar as it belonged to their age in a distinctive way. That no single idea, no system, no requirement is decisive for them follows from the fact that neither thinker expressed his epoch at its peak, that they constructed no world, nor any image of a passing world. They did not feel themselves to be a positive expression of their times; they rather expressed what it was negatively through their very being: an age absolutely rejected by them and seen through in its ruin. Their problem appeared to be to experience this epoch to the end in their own natures, to be it completely in order to overcome it. This happened at first involuntarily, but then consciously through the fact that they were not representatives of their epoch, but needling and scandalous *exceptions*. Let us look at this a little closer.

1. THEIR PROBLEM

Both had become aware of their *problem* by the end of their youth, even if unclearly. A decision which gripped the entire man, which sometimes was silent and no longer conscious, but which would return to force itself upon them, pushed them into a radical loneliness. Although without position, marriage, without any effective role in existence, they nevertheless appear as the great realists, who had an authentic feeling for the depths of reality.

2. PERCEPTION OF SUBSTANTIAL CHANGE IN ESSENCE OF MEN

They touched this reality in their fundamental experience of their epoch as ruins; looking back over centuries, back to the beginnings in Greek antiquity, they felt the end of this whole history. At the crucial point, they called attention to this moment, without wanting to survey the meaning and course of history as a whole.

Men have tried to understand this epoch in economic, technological, historico-political, and sociological terms. Kierkegaard and Nietzsche, on the other hand, thought they saw a change in the very substance of man.

Kierkegaard looked upon the whole of Christianity as it is today as upon an enormous deception in which God is held to be a fool. Such Christianity has nothing to do with that of the New Testament. There are only two ways:

either to maintain the deception through tricks and conceal the real conditions, and then everything comes to nothing; or honestly to confess the misery that in truth, today, not one single individual is born who can pass for a Christian in the sense of the New Testament. Not one of us is a Christian, but rather we live in a pious softening of Christianity. The confession will show if there is anything true left in this honesty, if it has the approval of Providence. If not, then everything must again be broken so that in this horror individuals can arise again who can support the Christianity of the New Testament.

Nietzsche expressed the historical situation of the epoch in one phrase: God is dead.

Thus, common to both, is an historical judgment on the very substance of their times. They saw before them Nothingness; both knew the substance of what had been lost, but neither willed Nothingness. If Kierkegaard presupposed the truth, or the possibility of the truth of Christianity, and Nietzsche, on the other hand, found in atheism not simply a loss but rather the greatest opportunity—still, what is common to both is a will toward the substance of Being, toward the nobility and value of man. They had no political program for reform, no program at all; they directed their attention to no single detail, but rather wanted to effect something through their thought which they foresaw in no clear detail. For Nietzsche, this indeterminateness was his "larger politics" at long range; for Kierkegaard, it was becoming Christian in the new way of indifference to all worldly being. Both in their relation to their epoch were possessed by the question of what will become of man.

3. MODERNITY OVERCOME

They are modernity itself in a somersaulting form. They ran it to the ground, and overcame it by living it through to the end. We can see how both experienced the distress of the epoch, not passively, but suicidally through totally doing what most only half did: first of all, in their endless reflection; and then, in opposition to this, in their drive toward the basic; and finally, in the way in which, as they sank into the bottomless, they grasped hold upon the Transcendent.

(i) *unlimited reflection.* The age of reflection has, since Fichte, been characterized as reasoning without restraint, as the dissolving of all authority, as the surrender of content which gives to thinking its measure, purpose, and meaning, so that from now on, without hindrance and as an indifferent play of the intellect, it can fill the world with noise and dust.

Kierkegaard and Nietzsche did not oppose reflection in order to annihilate it, but rather in order to overcome it by limitlessly engaging in it and mastering it. Man cannot sink back into an unreflective immediacy without losing himself; but he can go this way to the end, not destroying reflection, but rather coming to the basis in himself in the medium of reflection.

Their "infinite reflection" has, therefore, a twofold character. It can lead to a complete ruin just as well as it can become the condition of authentic Existenz. Both express this, perhaps Kierkegaard is the clearer of the two:

Reflection cannot exhaust or stop itself. It is faithless, since it hinders every decision. It is never finished and, in the end, can become "dialectical twaddle"; in this respect, he called it the poison of reflection. But that it is possible, indeed necessary, lies grounded in the endless ambiguity of all existence and action for us: anything can mean something else for reflection. This situation makes possible on one side a sophistry of existence, enables the Existenz-less esthete to profit, who merely wants to savor everything as an interesting novelty. Even if he should take the most decisive step, still he always holds before himself the possibility of reinterpreting everything, so that, in one blow, it is all changed. But on the other hand, this situation can be truly grasped by the knowledge that insofar as we are honest we live in a "sea of reflection where no one can call to another, where all buoys are dialectical."

Without infinite reflection we should fall into the quiet of the settled and established which, as something permanent in the world, would become absolute; that is, we should become superstitious. An atmosphere of bondage arises with such a settlement. Infinite reflection, therefore, is, precisely through its endlessly active dialectic, the condition of freedom. It breaks out of every prison of the finite. Only in its medium is there any possibility of an infinite passion arising out of immediate feeling which, because it is unquestioning, is still unfree. In infinite passion the immediate feeling, which is held fast and genuinely true throughout the questioning, is grasped as free.

But in order to prevent this freedom from becoming nothing through vacuous reflection, in order for it to fulfill itself, infinite reflection must strand itself. Then, for the first time, does it issue out of something real, or exhaust itself in the decision of faith and resolution. As untrue as the arbitrary and forced arrest of reflection is, so true is that basis by which reflection is mastered in the encounter of Existenz. Here Existenz is given to itself for the first time, so that it becomes master of infinite reflection through totally surrendering to it.

Reflection, which can just as well dissolve into nothing as become the condition of Existenz, is described as such and in the same way by both Kierkegaard and Nietzsche. Out of it, they have imparted an almost immeasurable wealth of thought in their works. This thinking, according to its own meaning, is possibility: it can indicate and prepare the way for the shipwreck, but cannot accomplish it.

Thus, in their thinking about the possibilities of man, both thinkers were aware of what they themselves were not in their thought. The awareness of possibilities, in analogy to poetry, is not a false, but rather a questioning and awakening reflection. Possibility is the form in which I permit myself to know about what I am not yet, and a preparation for being it.

Kierkegaard called his method most frequently, "an experimental psychology"; Nietzsche called his thought, "seductive."

Thus they left what they themselves were and what they ultimately thought concealed to the point of unrecognizability and, in its appearance, sunk into the incomprehensible. Kierkegaard's pseudonym writes: "The something which I am . . . is precisely a nothing." It gave him a high satisfaction to hold his "Existenz at that critical zero . . . between something and nothing, a mere perhaps." And Nietzsche willingly called himself a "philosopher of the dangerous perhaps."

Reflection is for both pre-eminently self-reflection. For them, the way to truth is through understanding oneself. But they both experienced how one's own substance can disappear this way, how the free, creative self-understanding can be replaced by a slavish rotation about one's own empirical existence. Kierkegaard knew the horror "of everything disappearing before a sick brooding over the tale of one's own miserable self." He sought for the way "between this devouring of oneself in observations as though one were the only man who had ever been, and the sorry comfort of a universal human shipwreck." He knew the "unhappy relativity in everything, the unending question about what I am." Nietzsche expressed it:

> Among a hundred mirrors
> before yourself false . . .
> strangled in your own net
> Self-knower!
> Self-executioner!
> crammed between two nothings,
> a question mark . . .

(ii) *drive toward the basic.* The age which could no longer find its way amidst the multiplicity of its reflections and rationalizing words pushed out of reflection toward bases. Kierkegaard and Nietzsche here too seem to be forerunners. Later generations sought the basic in general in articulateness, in the esthetic charm of the immediately striking, in a general simplification, in unreflective experience, in the existence of the things closest to us. To them, Kierkegaard and Nietzsche seem useful; for both lived consciously with a passionate love for the sources of human communicability.

They were creative in language to the degree that their works belong to the peaks of the literatures of their countries; and they knew it. They were creative in the thrilling way which made them among the most widely read authors, even though the content was of the same weight and their genuine comprehension of the same difficulty as that of any of the great philosophers. But both also knew the tendency of the verbal to become autonomous, and they despised the literary world.

Both were moved by music to the point of intoxication; but both warned of its seduction, and along with Plato and Augustine belonged to those who suspected it existentially.

Everywhere they created formulas of striking simplicity. But both were full of concern before that simplicity which, in order to give some deceptive support to the weak and mediocre, offered flat, spiritless simplifications in place of the genuine simplicity which was the result of the most complicated personal development, which, like Being itself, never had a single rational meaning. They warned, as no thinker before had, against taking their words too simply, words which seemed to stand there apodictically.

In fact, they went by the most radical way to the basic, but in such a fashion that the dialectical movement never stopped. Their seriousness was absorbed neither into an illusion of the dogmatic fixedness of some supposed basis, nor into the purposes of language, esthetic charm, and simplicity.

(iii) *arrest in Transcendence*. Both pursued a path which, for them, could not end short of a transcendental stop, for their reflections were not, like the usual reflections of modernity, stopped by the obvious limits of vital needs and interests. They, for whom it was a question of all or nothing, dared limitlessness. But this they could do only because from the very beginning onwards they were rooted in what was at the same time hidden from them: both, in their youth, spoke of an *unknown God*. Kierkegaard, even when twenty-five years old, wrote: "In spite of the fact that I am very far from understanding myself, I have . . . revered the unkown God." And Nietzsche at twenty years of age created his first unforgettable poem, "To the Unknown God":

> I would know Thee, Unknown,
> Thou who grips deep in my soul,
> wandering through my life like a storm,
> Thou inconceivable, my kin!
> I would know Thee, even serve Thee.

Never in their limitless reflection could they remain within the finite, conceivable, and therefore trivial; but just as little could they hold to reflection itself. Precisely because he had been thoroughly penetrated by reflection, Kierkegaard thought: "The religious understanding of myself has deserted me; I feel like an insect with which children are playing, so pitilessly does existence handle me." In his terrible loneliness, understood by and really bound to absolutely no one, he called to God: "God in heaven, if there were not some most inward center in a man where all this could be forgotten, who could hold out?"

Nietzsche was always conscious of moving on the sea of the infinite, of having given up land once and for all. He knew that, perhaps, neither Dante nor Spinoza knew his loneliness; somehow, they had God for company. But Nietzsche, empty in his loneliness, without men and without the ancient God, envisaged Zarathustra and meditated upon the eternal return, thoughts which left him as horrified as happy. He lived continually like someone mortally wounded. He suffered his problems. His thought is a self-arousal: "If I only had the courage to think all that I know." But, in this limitless reflecting, a deeply satisfying content was revealed which was in fact transcendent.

Thus both leaped toward Transcendence, but to a form of transcendence where practically no one could follow. Kierkegaard leaped to a Christianity which was conceived as an absurd paradox, as decision for utter world negation and martyrdom. Nietzsche leaped to the eternal return and supermen.

Thus the ideas, which were for Nietzsche himself the very deepest, can look empty to us; Kierkegaard's faith can look like a sinister alienation. If one takes the symbols of Nietzsche's religion literally, there is no longer any transcendental content in their will toward immanence: aside from the eternal cycle of things, there is the will to power, the affirmation of Being, the pleasure which "wills deep, deep eternity." Only with circumspection and by taking pains does a more essential content emerge. With Kierkegaard, who revivified the profound formulas of theology, it can seem like the peculiar art of perhaps a nonbeliever, forcing himself to believe.

The similarity of their thought is ever so much more striking precisely because of their apparent differences: the Christian belief of the one, and the atheism emphasized by the other. In an epoch of reflection, where what had really passed away seemed still to endure, but which actually lived in an absence of faith—rejecting faith and forcing oneself to believe belong together. The godless can appear to be a believer; the believer can appear as godless; both stand in the same dialectic.

What they brought forth in their existential thinking would not have been possible without a complete possession of tradition. Both were brought up with a classical education. Both were nurtured in Christian piety. Their tendencies are unthinkable without Christian origins. If they passionately opposed the stream of this tradition in the form which it had come to assume through the centuries, they also found an historical and, for them, indestructible arrest in these origins. They bound themselves to a basis which fulfilled their own belief: Kierkegaard to a Christianity of the New Testament as he understood it, and Nietzsche to a pre-Socratic Hellenism.

But nowhere is there any final stop for them, neither in finitude, nor in an explicitly grasped basis, nor in a determinately grasped Transcendence, nor in an historical tradition. It is as though their very being, experiencing the abandonment of the age to the end, shattered and, in the shattering itself, manifested a truth which otherwise would never have come to expression. If they won an unheard-of mastery over their own selves, they also were condemned to a worldless loneliness; they were as though pushed out.

4. THEIR BEING AS EXCEPTIONS

They were exceptions in every sense. Physically, their development was in retard of their character. Their faces disconcert one because of their relative unobtrusiveness. They do not impress one as types of human greatness. It is as if they both lacked something in sheer vitality. Or as though they were eternally young spirits, wandering through the world, without reality because without any real connection with the world.

Those who knew them felt attracted in an enigmatic way by their presence, as though elevated for a moment to a higher mode of being; but no one really loved them.

In the circumstances of their lives, one finds astonishing and alien features. They have been called simply insane.

They would be in fact objects for a psychiatric analysis, if that were not to the prejudice of the singular height of their thought and the nobility of their natures. Indeed, then they would first come to light. But any typical diagnosis or classification would certainly fail.

They cannot be classed under any earlier type (poet, philosopher, prophet, savior, genius). With them, a new form of human reality appears in history. They are, so to speak, representative destinies, sacrifices whose way out of the world leads to experiences for others. They are by the total staking of their whole natures like modern martyrs, which, however, they precisely denied being. Through their character as exceptions, they solved their problem.

Both are irreplaceable, as having dared to be shipwrecked. We orient ourselves by them. Through them we have intimations of something we could never have perceived without such sacrifices, of something that seems essential which even today we cannot adequately grasp. It is as if the Truth itself spoke, bringing an unrest into the depths of our consciousness of being.

Even in the external circumstances of their lives we find astonishing similarities. Both came to a sudden end in their forties. Shortly before, without knowledge of their approaching end, they both made public and passionate attacks: Kierkegaard on church Christianity and on dishonesty, Nietzsche on Christendom itself.

Both made literary reputations in their first publications; but then their new books followed unceasingly, and they had to print what they wrote at their own expense.

They also both had the fate of finding a response which however was without understanding. They were merely sensations in an age when nothing opposed them. The beauty and sparkle of language, the literary and poetic qualities, the aggressiveness of their matter all misled readers from their genuine intentions. Both, toward the end, were almost idolized by those with whom they had the least in common. The age that wanted to surpass itself could, so to speak, wear itself out in ideas casually selected out of them.

The modern world has nourished itself on them precisely in its negligence. Out of their reflection, instead of remaining in the seriousness of endless reflection, it made an instrument for sophistry in irresponsible talk. Their words, like their whole lives, were savored for their great esthetic charm. They dissolved what remained of connections among men, not to lead to the bases of true seriousness, but in order to prepare a free path for caprice. Thus their influence became utterly destructive, contrary to the meaning of their thought and being.

C. The ways in which they understood themselves: against interchangeability.

Their problem became clearer to them from their youth onward through a continually accompanying reflection. Both of them, at the end and in retrospect, gave us an indication of how they understood themselves through a total interpretation of their work. This interpretation remained convincing to the extent that we, today, in fact understand them as they wished to be understood. All their thought takes on a new sense beyond what is immediately comprehensible in it. This picture itself is inseparable from their work, for the fashion in which they understood themselves is not an accidental addition, but an essential feature of their total thought.

One of the motives in common for the comprehensive expression of their self-understanding is the will not to be mistaken for someone else. This was, they said, one of their deepest concerns, and out of it not only were they always seeking new forms of communication, but also they directly announced the total meaning as it appeared to them at the end. They always worked by all possible means to prepare a correct understanding of their work through the ambiguity of what they said.

1. THEIR SELF-CONSCIOUSNESS

They both had a clear perception of their epoch, seeing what was going on before them down to the smallest detail with a certitude that was overmastering: it was the end of a mode of life that had hung together for centuries. But they also perceived that no one else saw it, that they had an awareness of their epoch which no one else yet had, but which presently others, and finally all, would have. Thus they necessarily passed into an unprecedented intensity of *self-consciousness*. Their Existenz was in a very special state of affairs. It was not just a simple spiritual superiority which they must have noticed—Kierkegaard over everybody who encountered him, Nietzsche over most—but rather something monstrous which they made themselves into: unique, solitary world-historical destinies.

2. THEIR CONSCIOUSNESS OF FAILURE, OF EXCEPTIONALITY, OF LONELINESS

But this well-grounded self-consciousness, momentarily expressed and then suppressed again, is always with Kierkegaard moderated through the humility of his Christian attitude and, with both, is tempered by the psychological knowledge of their human failure. The astonishing thing with them again is that the precise mode of their failure is itself the condition of their distinctive greatness. For this greatness is not absolute greatness, but something that uniquely belongs to the situation of the epoch.

It is noteworthy how they both came to the same metaphors for this side of their natures. Nietzsche compared himself to the "scratchings which an unknown power makes on paper, in order to test a new pen." The positive value of his illness is his standing problem. Kierkegaard thought he indeed "would be erased by God's mighty hand, extinguished as an unsuccessful experiment." He felt like a sardine squashed against the sides of a can. The idea came to him that, "in every generation there are two or three who are sacrificed for the others, who discover in frightful suffering what others shall profit by." He felt like an "interjection in speaking, without influence upon the sentence," like a "letter which is printed upside down in the line." He compared himself with the paper notes in the financial crises of 1813, the year in which he was born. "There is something in me which might have been great, but due to the unfavorable market, I'm only worth a little."

Both were conscious of being exceptions. Kierkegaard developed a theory of the exception, through which he understood himself: he loved the universal, the human in men, but as something other, something denied to him. Nietzsche knew himself to be an exception, spoke "in favor of the exception, so long as it never becomes the rule." He required of philosophers "that they take care of the rule, since he is the exception."

Thus the last thing either wished was to become exemplary. Kierkegaard looked upon himself as "a sort of trial man." "In the human sense no one can imitate me. . . . I am a man as he could become in a crisis, an experimental rabbit, so to speak, for existence." Nietzsche turned away those who would follow him: "Follow not me, but you!"

This exceptionality, which was as excruciating to them as it was the unique requirement of their problem, they characterized—and here again they agree—as pure mentality, as though they were deprived of any authentic life. Kierkegaard said that he was "in almost every physical respect deprived of the conditions for being a whole man." He had never lived except as mind. He had never been a man: at very most, child and youth. He lacked "the animal side of humanity." His melancholy carried him almost to the "edge of imbecility" and was "something that he could conceal as long as he was independent, but made him useless for any service where he could not himself determine everything." Nietzsche experienced his own pure mentality as "through excess of light, through his radiance, condemned to be, not to love." He expressed it convulsively in the "Nightsong" of Zarathustra: "Light I am; ah! would that I were Night! . . . I live in my own light. . . ."

A terrible loneliness, bound up with their exceptionality, was common to both. Kierkegaard knew that he could have no friends. Nietzsche suffered his own growing loneliness in full consciousness to the limit where he felt he could endure it no longer. Again, the same image comes to both: Nietzsche compared himself to a fir tree on the heights overlooking an abyss: "Lonely! Who dares to be a guest here? Perhaps a bird of prey, gloating in the hair of the branches. . . ." And Kierkegaard: "Like a lonely fir tree, egoistically isolated, looking toward something higher, I stand there, throwing no shadow, only the wood dove building its nest in my branches."

3. PROVIDENCE AND CHANCE

In great contrast to the abandonment, failure, and contingency of their existence was the growing consciousness in the course of their lives of the meaning, sense, and necessity of all that happened to them.

Kierkegaard called it Providence. He recognized the divine in it: "That everything that happens, is said, goes on, and so forth, is portentous: the factual continually changes itself to mean something far higher." The factual for him is not something to abstract oneself from, but rather something to be penetrated until God himself gives the meaning. Even what he himself did became clear only later. It was "the extra which I do not owe to myself but to Providence. It shows itself continually in such a fashion that even what I do out of the greatest possible conviction, afterwards I understand far better."

Nietzsche called it chance. And he was concerned to use chance. For him "sublime chance" ruled existence. "The man of highest spirituality and power feels himself grown for every chance, but also inside a snowfall of contingencies." But this contingency increasingly took on for Nietzsche a remarkable meaning: "What you call chance—you yourself are that which befalls and astonishes you." Throughout his life, he found intimations of how chance events which were of the greatest importance to him carried a secret meaning, and in the end he wrote: "There is no more chance."

4. DANCING

At the limits of life's possibilities came not any heavy seriousness, but rather a complete lightness as the expression of their knowledge, and both used the image of the dance. In the last decade of his life Nietzsche, in ever-changing forms, used the dance as a metaphor for his thought, where it is original. And Kierkegaard said, "I have trained myself . . . always to be able to dance in the service of thought. . . . My life begins as soon as a difficulty shows up. Then dancing is easy. The thought of death is a nimble dancer. Everybody is too serious for me." Nietzsche saw his archenemy in the "spirit of seriousness" —in morals, science, purposefulness, etc. But to conquer seriousness meant not to reject it for the thoughtlessness of arbitrary caprice, but rather to pass through the most serious to an authentic soaring, the triumph of which is the free dance.

5. NO PROPHECY

The knowledge that they were exceptions prevented either from stepping forth as prophets. To be sure, they seem like those prophets who speak to us out of inaccessible depths but who speak in a contemporary way. Kierkegaard compared himself to a bird which foretells rain: "When in a generation, a thunderstorm begins to threaten, individuals like me appear." They are prophets who must conceal themselves as prophets. They were aware of their problem in a continual return from the extremities of their demands to a rejection of any idea which would make them models or ways of life. Kierkegaard repeated innumerable times that he was not an authority, or a prophet, apostle, or reformer, nor did he have the authority of position. His problem was to awaken men. He had a certain police talent, to be a spy in the service of the divinity. He uncovered, but he did not assert what should be done. Nietzsche wanted to "awaken the highest suspicion against himself," explaining that "to the humanity of a teacher belongs the duty of warning his students against himself." What he wanted he let Zarathustra say who left his disciples with: "Go away from me, and turn yourselves against me." And, even in *Ecce Homo*, Nietzsche says: "And finally, there is nothing in me of the founder of a religion. . . . I want no believers. . . . I have a terrible anxiety that some day, they will speak reverently of me. I will not be a saint, rather a Punch. Maybe I am Punch."

6. THE DEED

There is in both a confusing polarity between the appearance of an absolute and definite demand and, at the same time, shyness, withdrawal, the appearance of not betting anything. The Seductive, the Perhaps, the Possible is the manner of their discourse; an unreadiness to be a leader was their own attitude. But both lived in secret longing to bring salvation if they could, and if it could be done in human honesty. Accordingly, both toward the end of their lives became daring, desperate, and then, in utter calm, rose to public attack. From then on, the reticence of merely envisaging possibilities was given up for a will to act. Both made a similar attack: Kierkegaard attacked the Christianity of the church; Nietzsche attacked Christendom as such. Both acted with sudden force and merciless resolution. Both attacks were purely negative actions: deeds from truthfulness, not for the construction of a world.

III. MEANING OF THE PHILOSOPHICAL SITUATION PRODUCED BY KIERKEGAARD AND NIETZSCHE.

The significance of Kierkegaard and Nietzsche first becomes clear through what followed in consequence. The effect of both is immeasurably great, even greater in general thinking than in technical philosophy, but it is always ambiguous. What Kierkegaard really meant is clear neither in theology, nor in philosophy. Modern Protestant theology in Germany, when it is genuine, seems to stand under either a direct or indirect influence of Kierkegaard. But Kierkegaard with regard to practical consequences of his thought wrote in May, 1855, a pamphlet with the motto, "But at midnight there is a cry" (Matthew 25:6), where he says: "By ceasing to take part in the official worship of God as it now is . . . thou hast one guilt less, . . . thou dost not participate in treating God as a fool, calling it the Christianity of the New Testament, which it is not."

A. Ambiguity of both.

In modern philosophy several decisive themes have been developed through Kierkegaard. The most essential basic categories of contemporary philosophizing, at least in Germany, go back to Kierkegaard—Kierkegaard whose whole thought however appeared to dissolve all previous systematic philosophy, to reject speculation, and who, when he recognized philosophy, said at most: "Philosophy can pay attention to but cannot nourish us."

It might be that theology, like philosophy, when it follows Kierkegaard is masking something essential in order to use his ideas and formulas for its own totally different purposes.

It might be that within theology there is an unbelief which employs the refined Kierkegaardian intellectual techniques of dialectical paradox to set forth a kind of creed which can be understood, and which believes itself the genuine Christian faith.

It might be that philosophizing in the fashion of Kierkegaard secretly nourishes itself on the substance of Christianity, which it ignores in words.

The significance of Nietzsche is no clearer. His effect in Germany was like that of no other philosopher. But it seems as though every attitude, every world-view, every conviction claims him as authority. It might be that none of us really knows what this thought includes and does.

B. Their disordering influence.

The problem, therefore, for everyone who allows Kierkegaard and Nietzsche to influence him, is to become honest about how he really comes to terms with them, what they are to him, what he can make out of them.

Their common effect, to enchant and then to disillusion, to seize and then leave one standing unsatisfied as though one's hands and heart were left empty—such is only a clear expression of their own intention: that everything depends upon what their reader by his own inner action makes out of their communication, where there is no specific content as in the special sciences, works of art, philosophical systems, or some accepted prophecy. They deny every satisfaction.

C. The problem of philosophizing in relation to both.

In fact, they are exceptions and not models for followers. Whenever anyone has tried to imitate Kierkegaard or Nietzsche, if only in style, he has become ridiculous. What they did themselves at moments approaches the limit where the sublime passes into the ridiculous. What they did was only possible once. To be sure, everything great is unique, and can never be repeated identically. But there is something essentially different in our relation to this uniqueness: and this whether we live through them, and, by making them our own, revive them, or see them through the distance of an orientation which changes us but makes them more remote.

They abandon us without giving us any final goals and without posing any definite problems. Through them, each one can only become what he himself is. What their consequences are is not yet decided even today. The question is: how those of us shall live who are not exceptions but who are seeking our inner way in the light of these exceptions.

We are in that cultural situation where the application of this knowledge already contains the kernel of dishonesty. It is as though through them we were forced out of a certain thoughtlessness, which without them would have remained even in the study of great philosophers. We can no longer tranquilly proceed in the continuity of a traditional, intellectual education. For through Kierkegaard and Nietzsche a mode of existential experience has become effective, whose consequences on all sides have not yet come to light. They posed a question which is not yet clear but which one can feel; this question is still open. Through them we have become aware that for us there is no longer any self-evident foundation. There is no longer any secure background for our thought.

For the individual working with them, there are two equally great dangers: really to encounter them and not to take them seriously at all. Unavoidably, one's attitude toward them is ambivalent. Neither constructed a world, and both seemed to have destroyed everything; yet both were positive spirits. We must achieve a distinctively new relation to the creative thinker if we are really to approach them otherwise than we would any great man.

D. The question: What now?

With respect to our epoch and the thought of Kierkegaard and Nietzsche, if we pose the question, what now?

then Kierkegaard points in the direction of an absurd Christianity before which the world sinks away, and Nietzsche points to the distance, the indeterminate, which does not appear to be a substance out of which we can live. Nobody has accepted their answers; they are not ours. It is for us to see what will become of us through ourselves as we look upon them. This is, however, in no way to sketch out or establish anything in advance.

Thus we would err if we thought we could deduce what must now happen from a world-historical survey of the development of the human spirit. We do not stand outside like a god who can survey the whole at a glance. For us, the present cannot be replaced by some supposed world history out of which our situation and problems would emerge. And this lecture has no intention of surveying the whole, but rather of making the present situation perceptible by reflecting upon the past. Nobody knows where man and his thinking are going. Since existence, man, and his world are not at an end, a completed philosophy is as little possible as an anticipation of the whole. We men have plans with finite ends, but something else always comes out which no one willed. In the same way, philosophizing is an act which works upon the inwardness of man, but whose final meaning he cannot know. Thus the contemporary problem is not to be deduced from some a priori whole; rather it is to be brought to consciousness out of a basis which is now experienced and out of a content still unclearly willed. Philosophy as thought is always a consciousness of Being which is complete for this moment, but which knows it has no final permanence in its form of expression.

E. The problem we have abstracted from the situation: Reason and Existenz.

Instead of some supposed total view of the actual and cultural situation, rather we philosophize in consciousness of a situation which again leads to the final limits and bases of the human reality. Today, no one can completely and clearly develop the intellectual problems that grow out of such a situation. We live, so to speak, in a seething cauldron of possibilities, continually threatened by confusion, but always ready in spite of everything to rise up again. In philosophizing, we must always be ready, out of the present questioning, to elicit those ideas which bring forth what is real to us: that is, our humanity. These ideas are possible when the horizon remains unlimited, the realities clear, and the real questions manifest. Out of such problems which force themselves upon thought, I have selected one for the next three lectures. The ancient philosophical problem, which appears in the relation of the rational to the non-rational, must be seen in a new light through an appropriation of the tradition with our eyes upon Kierkegaard and Nietzsche.

We formulate this fundamental problem as that of reason and Existenz. This abbreviated formula signifies no antithesis: rather a connection which at the same time points beyond itself.

The words "reason" and "Existenz" are chosen because for us they express in the most penetrating and pure form the problem of the clarification of the dark, the grasping of the bases out of which we live, presupposing no transparency, but demanding the maximum of rationality.

The word "reason" has here its Kantian scope, clarity and truth. The word "Existenz" through Kierkegaard has taken on a sense through which we look into infinite depths at what defies all determinate knowledge. The word is not to be taken in its worn-out sense as one of the many synonyms for "being"; it either means nothing, or is to be taken with its Kierkegaardian claims.

What we shall undertake in the next three lectures may seem to move around other themes. But in common, they shall strive to grasp in the form of logically conceived questions the meaning of what is closest to life. Philosophy, wherever it is successful, consists of those unique ideas in which logical abstractness and the actual present become, so to speak, identical. The basic drives of living philosophy can express themselves truly only in purely formal thought. There are intellectual operations which through comprehension and cooperation can bring about an inner act of the entire man: the bringing forth of oneself out of possibilities in thought so as to apprehend Being in empirical existence.

If my lectures do not come even close to satisfying these high demands, it is still essential that the ideal of one's concerns be recognized. One can take courage to try to do that which passes beyond his strength from the fact that it is a human problem, and man is that creature which poses problems beyond his powers. And also from this, that whoever even once thought he heard softly the authentic philosophic note can never tire of trying to communicate it.

The Fifth Lecture shall take up again the theme of this one. It will in reference to the previously developed ideas take up the problems of contemporary philosophy in a situation decisively determined by Kierkegaard and Nietzsche.

second lecture

THE ENCOMPASSING

INTRODUCTION: THE MEANING OF PHILOSOPHICAL LOGIC.

One possible way of philosophizing is the movement of philosophical logic in those acts of thought which formally represent the various modes of Being. Since we shall make an initial investigation of this possibility in the three middle lectures, here we shall ignore all concrete philosophizing, that is, the development of particular physical, existential, or metaphysical subjects. Rather we shall be concerned with the horizons and forms within which philosophical contents can be established without deception—horizons which became visible when our humanity was pushed to its very limits by Kierkegaard and Nietzsche.

A. 1. The Question of the Encompassing.

In order to see most clearly into what is true and real, into what is no longer fastened to any particular thing or colored by any particular atmosphere, we must push into the widest range of the possible. And then we experience the following: everything that is an object for us, even though it be the greatest, is still always within another, is not yet all. Wherever we arrive, the horizon which includes the attained itself goes further and forces us to give up any final rest. We can secure no standpoint from which a closed whole of Being would be surveyable, nor any sequence of standpoints through whose totality Being would be given even indirectly.

We always live and think within a horizon. But the very fact that it is a horizon indicates something further which again surrounds the given horizon. From this situation arises the question about the Encompassing. The Encompassing is not a horizon within which every determinate mode of Being and truth emerges for us, but rather that within which every particular horizon is enclosed as in something absolutely comprehensive which is no longer visible as a horizon at all.

2. The Two Modes of the Encompassing.

The Encompassing appears and disappears for us in two opposed perspectives: either as Being itself, in and through which we are—or else as the Encompassing which we ourselves are, and in which every mode of Being appears to us. The latter would be as the medium or condition under which all Being appears as Being for us. In neither case is the Encompassing the sum of some provisional kinds of being, a part of whose contents we know, but rather it is the whole as the most extreme, self-supporting ground of Being, whether it is Being in itself, or Being as it is for us.

All of our natural knowledge and dealings with things lies between these final and no longer conditioned bases of encompassing Being. The Encompassing never appears as an object in experience, nor as an explicit theme of thinking, and therefore might seem to be empty. But precisely here is where the possibility for our deepest insight into Being arises, whereas all other knowledge about Being is merely knowledge of particular, individual being.

Knowledge of the many always leads to distraction. One runs into the infinite unless one arbitrarily sets a limit by some unquestioned purpose or contingent interest. And in that case, precisely at these limits, one always runs into bewildering difficulties. Knowledge about the Encompassing would put all the knowable as a whole under such conditions.

B. Historical Reflections on this Basic Philosophical Question.

To seek this Being itself beyond the endlessness of the particular and partial was the first, and is always the new way, of philosophizing. This is what Aristotle meant when he said, "And indeed the question which was raised of old and is raised now and always, and is ever the subject of doubt is, what is Being" (*Metaphysics*, 1028 b). Schelling, too, held it to be "the oldest and most correct explanation of what philosophy is . . . that it is the science of Being. But to find what Being is, that is, true Being—that is the difficulty: *hoc opus, hic labor est*" (II, 3, 76). That from the beginning of philosophy up to the present this question continually recurs might arouse confidence in the abiding, fundamental meaning of philosophy throughout its almost endless multiplicities of appearance.

The first difficulty is to understand the question correctly. And the correct understanding of the question shows itself in the answer, shows itself in the degree to which we can appropriate the truth and reject the falsity of historically given questions and answers in their basic and connected meaning. But such a task, in the light of the enormous projects and catastrophes of philosophy, can be accomplished neither through a collection of ideas, nor through forcibly limiting it to some supposedly basic feature to which everything is to be added. We must presuppose a philosophic attitude whose passion for the truth, in a continuing attempt to grasp one's own Existenz, achieves awareness of an unlimited range by continued questioning. In such an unlimited range, the simplicity of the origin may finally be given truly.

Of the two approaches to Being as the Encompassing, the most usual and most natural way for every beginning philosophy is toward Being in itself, conceived as Nature, World, or God. However, we shall approach it from the other, and since Kant unavoidable, way; we shall search into the Encompassing which we are. Although we know, or at least take into account, the fact that the Encompassing which we are is in no wise Being itself, still this can be seen in critical purity only after we have gone to the end of the path opened up by Kant.

I. THE ENCOMPASSING WHICH WE ARE: EMPIRICAL EXISTENCE, CONSCIOUSNESS AS SUCH, SPIRIT.

Whether we call the Encompassing which we are our empirical existence, consciousness as such, or spirit, in no case can it be grasped as though it were something in the world which appeared before us. Rather it is that in which all other things appear to us. In general, we do not appropriately cognize it as an object; rather we become aware of it as a limit. This is confirmed when we abandon the determinate, clear—because objective—knowledge which is directed to particular things distinguishable from other things. We should like, so to speak, to stand outside ourselves in order to look and see what we are; but in this supposed looking we are and always remain enclosed within that at which we are looking.

Let us consider for a moment some beginnings from which, by repeated questioning, the Encompassing can be conceived. I am, first of all, an empirical existent. Empirical existence means the actual taken comprehensively, which immediately shows itself to empirical consciousness in the particularities of matter, living body, and soul, but which, as such particularities, is no longer the Encompassing of empirical existence. Everything which is empirically actual for me must in some sense be actual as a part of my being, as, for example, in the continually perceptible presence of my body as it is touched, altered, or as it is perceiving.

Empirical existence, as the overpowering Other which determines me, is the world. The Encompassing of empirical existence which I am when made into an object also becomes something alien like the world. As soon as our empirical existence becomes an object for investigation, we become absorbed into the being of the world which is that incomprehensible Other, Nature. In this fashion we are apprehended only as one sort of being among others, not yet as properly human. Knowledge of the Encompassing of empirical existence with which we are united removes from particular sciences the claim of grasping us as a whole.

Although I can never comprehend my empirical existence as an Encompassing, but only particular empirical forms like matter, life, and soul which I can never reduce back to a single principle, still I stand in the continuous presence of this embracing empirical reality. But even if we know the body, life, the soul, and consciousness merely as they become objectively accessible to us, even here we can, so to speak, see through them all back to that Encompassing of empirical existence with which we are one and which becomes only particularized in every physical, biological, and psychological object, but which, as such, is no longer the Encompassing. Thus the empirical awareness which I have as a living actuality is, as such, not constitutive by itself of that Encompassing which I am as an empirical existent.

The second mode of the Encompassing which I am is consciousness as such. Only what appears to our consciousness as experienceable, as an object, has being for us. What does not appear to consciousness, what can in no wise touch our cognition, is as good as nothing for us. Hence, everything which exists for us must take on that form in which it can be thought or experienced by consciousness. It must in some fashion appear in the form of an object; it must become present through some temporal act of consciousness; it must become articulated and thereby communicable through its thinkability. That all being for us must appear in those forms under which it can enter into consciousness is what imprisons us in the Encompassing of thinkability. But we can make clear its limits and, with this consciousness of limits, become open to the possibility of the Other which we do not know. Consciousness has two meanings however: (i) we are conscious as living existents and, as such, are not yet or no longer encompassing. This consciousness is carried by life itself, the unconscious ground of what we consciously experience. As living existents which we are *in* an absolute Encompassing of empirical existence, we become possible objects of empirical investigation for ourselves. We find ourselves divided into groups of races and into those always particular individualities into which this form of reality divides itself. However, we are not only countless single consciousnesses, which are more or less similar to one another; we are also therein (ii) consciousness as such. Through such consciousness we think we can refer to Being, not only in similar ways of perception and feeling, but in an identical way. Contrasting with empirical consciousness, this is the other sense of consciousness which we are as Encompassing. There is a leap between the multiplicity of subjective consciousnesses and the universal validity of that true consciousness which can only be *one*. As the consciousness of living beings, we are split into the multiplicity of endless particular realities, imprisoned in the narrowness of the individual and not encompassing. As consciousness in general, we participate in an inactuality, the universally valid truth, and, as such consciousness, are an infinite Encompassing. As a conscious living actuality, we are always a mere kind, even a unique individual enclosed within its own individuality. But we participate in the Encompassing through the possibility of knowledge and through the possibility of common knowledge of Being in every form in which it appears to consciousness. And, indeed, we participate, not only in the validity of the knowable, but also in a universally recognized, formal lawfulness in willing, action, and feeling. So defined, truth is timeless, and our temporal actuality is a more or less complete actualization of this timeless permanence.

This sharp separation, however, between the actuality of living consciousness in its temporal process and the inactuality of consciousness in general, as the site of the timeless meaning of the one common truth, is not absolute. Rather it is an abstraction which can be transcended through the clarification of the Encompassing. The actual existence of this timeless meaning insofar as it is something produced, something temporal, which grasps and moves itself, is a new sense of the Encompassing, and this is called spirit.

Spirit is the third mode of the Encompassing which we are. Out of the origins of its being, spirit is the totality of intelligible thought, action, and feeling—a totality which is not a closed object for knowledge but remains Idea. Although spirit is necessarily oriented to the truth of consciousness as such, as well as to the actuality of its Other (Nature as known and used), yet in both directions it is moved by Ideas which bring everything into clarity and connection. Spirit is the comprehensive reality of activity which is actualized by itself and by what it encounters in a world which is always given yet always being changed. It is the process of fusing and reconstructing all totalities in a present which is never finished yet always fulfilled. It is always on its way toward a possible completion of empirical existence where universality, the whole, and every particular would all be members of a totality. Out of a continuously actual and continuously fragmenting whole, it pushes forward, creating again and again out of its contemporary origins its own possible reality. Since it pushes toward the whole, spirit would preserve, enhance, and relate everything to everything else, exclude nothing, and give to everything its place and limits.

Spirit, in contrast to the abstraction of timeless consciousness as such, is again a temporal process, and as such it is comparable to empirical existence. But, as distinguished from this latter, it moves by a reflexivity of knowledge instead of by some merely biologico-psychological process. Understood from within and not capable of being investigated as a natural object, spirit is always directed toward the universality of consciousness as such. Thus it is a grasping of itself, a working upon itself through denial and approval. It produces itself by struggling with itself.

As mere empirical existence and as spirit, we are an encompassing reality. But as empirical existence, we are unconsciously bound to our ultimate bases in matter, life, and the psyche. When we understand ourselves as objects in this horizon, we see ourselves in an infinite, and only from the outside. We become split from one another, and only as thus split are we objects of scientific investigation (as matter, living beings, psyches). But as spirit we are consciously related to everything which is comprehensible to us. We transform the world and ourselves into the intelligible, which encloses totalities. As objects in this mode of the Encompassing, we know ourselves from within as the one, unique, all-embracing reality which is wholly spirit and only spirit.

The distinctions of empirical existence, consciousness as such, and spirit do not imply separable facts. Rather they represent three starting points through which we can come to feel that comprehensive Being which we are and in which all Being and everything scientifically investigable appears.

These three modes taken individually are not yet the Encompassing as we represent it. Consciousness as such, the location of universally valid truth, is in itself nothing independent. On one side, it points to its basis in empirical existence. On the other it points to spirit, the power it must let itself be dominated by if it would attain meaning and totality. In itself, consciousness as such is an unreal articulation of the Encompassing. Through it, the Encompassing is differentiated into those modes according to one of which the Encompassing can become individuated and knowable as empirical natural processes, and, according to the other of which it is understandable, a self-transparent, totalizing reality or Freedom. Empirical existence and spirit produce forms of reality; consciousness as such is the form in which we envisage the Encompassing as the condition of the universally valid and communicable.

II. THE ENCOMPASSING AS BEING ITSELF; WORLD AND TRANSCENDENCE.

We pass beyond the Encompassing which we are (empirical existence, consciousness as such, and spirit) when we ask whether this whole is Being itself.

If Being itself is that in which everything that is for us must become present, then it might be thought that this appearance-for-us is in fact all Being. Thus Nietzsche, who conceived all Being as interpretation and our being as interpretative, wanted to reject any further being as an illusory otherworld. But the question does not stop with the limits of our knowledge of things, nor in the inwardness of the limiting consciousness of the Encompassing which we are. Rather this Encompassing which I am and know as empirical existence, consciousness as such, and spirit, is not conceivable in itself but refers beyond itself. The Encompassing which we are is not Being itself, but rather the genuine appearance in the Encompassing of Being itself.

This Being itself which we feel as indicated at the limits, and which therefore is the last thing we reach through questioning from our situation, is in itself the first. It is not made by us, is not interpretation, and is not an object. Rather it itself brings forth our questioning and permits it no rest.

The Encompassing which we are has one of its limits in

fact. Even though we create the form of everything that we know, since it must appear to us in those modes according to which it can become an object, yet knowledge can not create the least particle of dust in its empirical existence. In the same way, Being itself is that which shows an immeasurable number of appearances to inquiry, but it itself always recedes and only manifests itself indirectly as that determinate empirical existence we encounter in the progress of our experiences and in the regularity of processes in all their particularity. We call it the World.

The Encompassing which we are has its other limit in the question through which it is. Being itself is the Transcendence which shows itself to no investigative experience, not even indirectly. It is that which as the absolute Encompassing just as certainly "is" as it remains unseen and unknown.

III. EXISTENZ, ANIMATION AND GROUND OF ALL MODES OF THE ENCOMPASSING.

Any philosopher who is not lost in the perspective of the conceptual but wishes to push toward genuine Being feels a deep dissatisfaction looking at all the hitherto mentioned modes of the Encompassing. He knows too little in the vast superfluity of apparently immeasurable multiplicities toward which he is directed. He can not find Being itself in all the dimensions of an Encompassing so conceived. He is liberated into a vastness where Being becomes void. The Transcendent seems to be merely an unknowable which makes no difference, and the spirit comes to seem like a sublime whole, but one in which each individual in his deepest inwardness almost seems to have disappeared.

The central point of philosophizing is first reached in the awareness of potential Existenz.

Existenz is the Encompassing, not in the sense of the vastness of a horizon of all horizons, but rather in the sense of a fundamental origin, the condition of selfhood without which all the vastness of Being becomes a desert. Existenz, although never itself becoming an object or form, carries the meaning of every mode of the Encompassing.

While mere empirical existence, consciousness as such, and spirit all appear in the world and become scientifically investigable realities, Existenz is the object of no science. In spite of which, we find here the very axis about which everything in the world turns if it is to have any genuine meaning for us.

At first Existenz seems to be a new narrowing, for it is always merely one among others. It might appear as though the spaciousness of the Encompassing had been contracted into the uniqueness of the individual self which, in contrast to the reality of encompassing spirit, looks like the emptiness of a point. But this contracted point lodged, so to speak, in the body of empirical existence, in this particular consciousness, and in this spirit, is, in fact, the sole possible revelation of the depths of Being as historicity. In all modes of the Encompassing, the self can become genuinely certain of itself only as Existenz.

If we first contrast Existenz with consciousness as such, it becomes the hidden ground in me to which Transcendence is first revealed. The Encompassing which we are exists only in relation to something other than itself. Thus, as I am conscious only insofar as I have something else as an objective being before me by which I then am determined and with which I am concerned, so also I am Existenz only as I know Transcendence as the power through which I genuinely am myself. The Other is either the being which is in the world for consciousness as such, or it is Transcendence for Existenz. This twofold Other first becomes clear through the inwardness of Existenz. Without Existenz the meaning of Transcendence is lost. It remains only something indifferent and not to be known, something supposed to be at the bottom of things, something excogitated, or, perhaps for our animal consciousness, something weird or terrifying plunging it into superstition and anxiety, a subject to be investigated psychologically and removed through a rational insight into the factual by consciousness as such. Only through Existenz can Transcendence become present without supersition, as the genuine reality which to itself never disappears.

Further, Existenz is like the counterpart to spirit. Spirit is the will to become *whole;* potential Existenz is the will to be authentic. Spirit is intelligible throughout, coming to itself in the whole; but Existenz is the unintelligible, standing by and against other Existenzen, breaking up every whole and never reaching any real totality. For spirit, a final transparency would be the origin of Being; Existenz on the other hand remains in all clarity of spirit as the irremediably dark origin. Spirit lets everything disappear and vanish into universality and totality. The individual as spirit is not himself but, so to speak, the unity of contingent individuals and of the necessary universal. Existenz however is irreducibly in another; it is the absolutely firm, the irreplaceable, and therefore, as against all mere empirical existence, consciousness as such, and spirit, it is authentic being before Transcendence to which alone it surrenders itself without reservation.

Spirit wants to grasp the individual either as an example of a universal or as a part of a whole. On the other hand, Existenz, as the possibility of decision derivable from no universal validity, is an origin in time, is the individual as historicity. It is the apprehension of timelessness through temporality, not through universal concepts.

Spirit is historical by representing itself in retrospect as a transparent totality. Existenz is historical as eternity in time, as the absolute historicity of its concrete empirical existence in a spiritual opacity which is never removed. But Existenz is not merely this incompletion and perversity in all temporal existence, which, as such, must always expand and change into some spiritual totality, but rather temporal existence thoroughly and authentically penetrated: the paradox of the unity of temporality and eternity.

Spirit in its immediacy is the *potential Idea*, whose universality unfolds into full clarity. Existenz in its immediacy, on the other hand, is its historicity in relation to Transcendence, i.e., the irremovable immediacy of its faith.

The faith of spirit is the life of the universal Idea, where *Thought is Being* ultimately is valid. The faith of Existenz, however, is the Absolute in Existenz itself on which everything for it rests, in which spirit, consciousness as such, and empirical existence are all bound together and decided, where for the first time there is both impulse and goal; here Kierkegaard's proposition, "Faith is Being," applies.

When Existenz understands itself, it is not like my understanding of another, nor the sort of understanding whose contents can be abstracted from the person understanding, nor a sort of looking at; rather it is an origin which itself first arises in its own self-clarification. It is not like sharing in something else, but is at once the understanding and the being of what is understood. It is not understanding through universals, but moves above such understanding in the medium of spirit to become an understanding without any generalization in the absolute present, in deed, in love, and in every form of absolute consciousness. It is the difference between the love of another, which I understand but yet never really understand, and my own love, which I understand because I am that love. Or, in other words, the difference between understanding other things by empathy as process or experience, and understanding myself as unique since I know myself before Transcendence.

When we compare Existenz with consciousness as such, spirit, or any other mode of the Encompassing, the same thing appears: without Existenz everything seems empty, hollowed out, without ground, fake, because everything has turned into endless masks, mere possibilities, or mere empirical existence.

IV. REASON: THE BOND BETWEEN THE VARIOUS MODES OF THE ENCOMPASSING.

We have seen as modes of the Encompassing:

a) Being as the Other, which was either World (empirical existence which can be investigated in a universally valid way) or Transcendence (as Being in itself).

b) The Being of the Encompassing which we are, which was either our empirical existence (the still indeterminate, comprehensive actuality), or consciousness as such (the site of all objective and intelligible validities for us), or spirit (the single whole of coherent movement of consciousness as it is activated by Ideas).

But for the source from which all these modes of the Encompassing receive animation and for which they speak, we touched upon Existenz, the dark ground of selfhood, the concealment out of which I come to encounter myself and for which Transcendence first becomes real.

Inextricably bound to Existenz is something else which concerns the connection of all these modes of the Encompassing. This is no new whole, but rather a continuing demand and movement. It is not a mode through which the Encompassing appears, but rather the *bond* which unites all modes of the Encompassing; it is called reason.

There is a question as to what "reason" means in the history of philosophy, how it comprehended itself, what it meant for Kierkegaard and Nietzsche, what they meant when they both trusted and mistrusted it. The clarification of the modes of the Encompassing must go into the ambiguity of what has passed for reason.

If reason means clear, objective thinking, the transformation of the opaque into the transparent, then it is nothing more than the Encompassing of consciousness as such. So considered, it would be better to call it, in accordance with the tradition of German idealism, understanding [Verstand].

If reason means the way to *totalities*, the life of the Idea, then it is the Encompassing of *spirit*.

But if reason means the pre-eminence of thought in all modes of the Encompassing, then more is included than mere thinking. It is then what goes beyond all limits, the omnipresent demand of thought, that not only grasps what is universally valid and is an *ens rationis* in the sense of being a law or principle of order of some process, but also brings to light the Other, stands before the absolutely counter-rational, touching it and bringing it, too, into being. Reason, through the pre-eminence of thought, can bring all the modes of the Encompassing to light by continually transcending limits, without itself being an Encompassing like them. It is, so to speak, like the final authentic Encompassing which continually must withdraw and remain inconceivable except in those modes of the Encompassing in which it moves.

Reason of itself is no source; but, as it is an encompassing bond, it is like a source in which all sources first come to light. It is the unrest which permits acquiescence in nothing; it forces a break with the immediacy of the unconscious in every mode of the Encompassing which we are. It pushes on continually. But it is also that which can effect the great peace, not the peace of a self-confident rational whole, but that of Being itself opened up to us through reason.

Reason is the inextinguishable impulse to philosophize with whose destruction reason itself is destroyed. This impulse is to achieve reason, to restore reason; it is that reason which always rises clearer from all the deviations and narrowings of so-called "reason" and which can acknowledge the justice of objections to reason and set their limits.

Reason should not get caught within any mode of the Encompassing: not in empirical existence to favor a will-to-exist which in its very narrowness asserts itself purposively yet blindly; nor in consciousness as such in favor of endless validities which are indifferent to us; nor in spirit in favor of a self-enclosed, harmonious totality which can be contemplated but not lived.

Reason is always too little when it is enclosed within final and determinate forms, and it is always too much when it appears as a self-sufficient substitute.

With the rational attitude I desire unlimited clarity; I try to know scientifically, to grasp the empirically real and the compelling validities of the thinkable; but at the same time, I live with an awareness of the limits of scientific penetrability and of clarity in general; however, I push forward from all sources in all modes of the Encompassing toward a universal unfolding of them in thought and reject above all thoughtlessness.

But reason itself is no timeless permanence; it is neither a quiet realm of truth (such as the contents of scientific cognition whose validity does not change although their attainment is an endless and restless movement); nor is it Being itself. Neither is it the mere moment of some chance thought. Rather it is the binding, recollecting, and progressive power whose contents are always derived from its own limits and which passes beyond every one of these limits, expressing perpetual dissatisfaction. It appears in all forms of the modes of the Encompassing yet seems to be nothing itself, a bond which does not rest upon itself but always on something else out of which reason produces both what it itself is and what it can be.

Reason drives toward unity, but it is not satisfied either with the one level of knowable accuracies for consciousness as such, or with the great effective unities of spirit. It goes along just as well with Existenz where the latter breaks through these unities, and so reason is again present in order to bring Existenzen separated by an abyss of absolute distance together into communication.

Its essence seems to be the universal, that which pushes

toward law and order or is identical with it. But it remains a possibility in Existenz even when these fail. Reason is itself still the only thing by and for which the chaos of the negative in its passion for Night preserves its mode of potential Existenz, a reason which otherwise would be surrendered to what is absolutely alien at these extreme limits.

V. REASON AND EXISTENZ.

The great poles of our being, which encounter one another in every mode of the Encompassing, are thus reason and Existenz. They are inseparable. Each disappears with the disappearance of the other. Reason should not surrender to Existenz to produce an isolating defiance which resists communication in despair. Existenz should not surrender to reason in favor of a transparency which is substituted for substantial reality.

Existenz only becomes clear through reason; reason only has content through Existenz.

There is an impulse in reason to move out of the immobility and endless triviality of the merely correct into a living bond through the totality of the ideas of the spirit, and out of these toward Existenz as that which supports and first gives authentic being to the spirit.

Reason is oriented toward its Other, toward the content of the Existenz which supports it, which clarifies itself in reason, and which gives decisive impulses to reason. Reason without content would be mere understanding, without any basis as reason. And, as the concepts of the understanding are empty without intuition, so reason is hollow without Existenz. Reason is not itself as mere understanding, but only in the acts of potential Existenz.

But Existenz is also oriented toward an Other. It is related to Transcendence through which it first becomes an independent cause in the world; for Existenz did not create itself. Without Transcendence, Existenz becomes a sterile, loveless, and demonic defiance. Existenz, oriented to reason through whose clarity it first experiences unrest and the appeal of Transcendence, under the needling questioning of reason first comes into its own authentic movement. Without reason, Existenz is inactive, sleeping, and as though not there.

Thus reason and Existenz are not two opposed powers which struggle with one another for victory. Each exists only through the other. They mutually develop one another and find through one another clarity and reality.

Although they never combine into an ultimate whole, every genuine accomplishment is whole only through them.

Reason without Existenz even in the richest possible field finally passes into an indifferent thinking, a merely intellectual movement of consciousness as such, or into a dialectic of the spirit. And as it slips away into intellectual universality without the binding root of its historicity, it ceases to be reason.

Irrational Existenz which rests upon feeling, experiencing, unquestioned impulse, instinct, or whim, ends up as blind violence, and therewith falls under the empirical laws which govern these actual forces. Without historicity, lost in the mere particularities of contingent empirical existence in a self-assertion unrelated to Transcendence, it ceases to be Existenz.

Each without the other loses the genuine continuity of Being and, therefore, the reliability which, although it can not be calculated, is nevertheless appropriate to genuine reason and Existenz. They separate themselves from one another only to become violent powers lacking any communication. In isolation they no longer mean what they should; only formulas without either basis or purpose remain, in a narrowing sphere of empirical existence. There, through a veil of justifications which are no longer true and no longer believed, they are simply the means of expression for mutually destructive empirical existents.

But there is rest nowhere in temporal existence. Rather

there is always movement issuing forth from the ultimate substantial ground—movement in the tension between the individual and the universal, between the actual and the total range of the possible, between the unquestionable immediacy of existential faith and the infinite movement of reason.

VI. REFLECTIONS ON THE SIGNIFICANCE OF THE FORM OF THIS BASIC IDEA.

After this survey of how we think of the modes of the Encompassing which we are and which Being itself is, and the polarity of reason and Existenz, let us now reflect on what such ideas, formally considered, can and can not mean —ideas whose development has given rise to whole philosophies.

Our knowledge of objects in the world has the form of relating them to one another and deriving them from one another. What appears to us is understood by understanding its relation to something else. But where, in philosophizing, we are concerned with the Encompassing, it is clear that we are dealing with something which can not be understood like some object in the world; more especially, we find that the modes of the Encompassing can not be derived from some particular which appears in them. For example: if we call the Encompassing thought, we can not derive thought itself from anything which can be thought of. Or if the Encompassing is our consciousness, it can not be derived from anything which appears to this consciousness. Or if it is the Whole, it can not be derived from any individual, be it ever so comprehensive. Or if it is empirical existence, then as such it can never be derived from any determinate, objectively known empirical thing. If it is reason, then we can not derive it from the non-rational. Or if it is Existenz, it can not be derived from any mode of the Encompassing, let alone one of its contents. In short, our being can never be derived from anything which appears to us; I myself can never be understood through anything which I encounter.

Just as little can Being in itself be derived from any being which we know. If we call it Being, it can never be derived from the multiplicity of beings. If it is Being in itself, it can never be derived from appearance. If it is Transcendence, we find we can never derive the absolute from the objective, actual, or empirically existent. There always arises in thinking man that which passes beyond everything of which he thinks.

In philosophy there has also been a contrary tendency to deduce from Being as such, as the Encompassing was regarded, the particular things we objectively know—to deduce the whole world, ourselves included, from a philosophically cognized origin, just as we grasp things in the world through their causes. This is again always a radical error which destroys philosophizing itself. For the Encompassing can never be known as a particular something from which other things can be deduced. Every object of thought, be it ever so comprehensive, every conceived whole, every objectively conceived Encompassing, remains as an object merely an individual, for it has other objects outside it and also stands over against us. The Encompassing itself, whether it be the Encompassing which we are or Being in itself, escapes from every determinate objectivity. Insofar as we are that Encompassing, it can only be illuminated; insofar as it is thought of as Being in itself, it is apprehended by inquiry into its infinite appearance; insofar as it speaks as Transcendence it is heard by absolute, historical Existenz.

Therefore, since the Encompassing is in no form known in itself, we can not deduce from it the being which appears to us. That could only occur if the Encompassing were previously known in itself. These false derivations proceed as though they had already cognitively mastered Being itself.

These deductions from one principle, perhaps in the form of a deduction of all categories of the thinkable and of whatever we can encounter in the world, are always merely relative derivations of individual groups in their connections. An exhaustive deduction has never succeeded and never can succeed. The attempt, however, has the value of sharpening our awareness of our limits.

Deductions of actual occurrences from theories of some fundamental reality construct models, but they never succeed in grasping anything except limited realities, mere aspects of empirical existence. They prove themselves to be functions of an endlessly progressive knowing; but they are never what in intention they might well like to be: cognition of the real in itself.

The deduction of the whole world including ourselves from Transcendence (by emanation, evolution, causality, etc.) is imaginary. The idea of creation is the expression of a primal secret, of an inconceivability, the subversion of the question through an uncaused cause.

However the Encompassing is conceived, the idea seems for a moment to achieve stability when it appears as an object for scientific research. This actually occurs in all modes of the Encompassing. The error lies in trying to secure as a content for knowledge what is true only as a limit for consciousness and a demand of the self.

The Encompassing in the form of empirical existence, consciousness as such, or spirit becomes an apparent object for anthropology, psychology, sociology, and the humanistic sciences. These sciences investigate human phenomena in the world, but in such a fashion that what they grasp is precisely not the encompassing reality of this kind of being, a reality which is always present to it even though unrecognized. No history or sociology of religion has arrived in what they call religion at that which was the Existenz itself of men. They can only consider religion according to its factual character, observe how it emerges into observable reality with a leap which is incomprehensible. All these sciences push toward something which is precisely what they can never reach. They have the fascination of being concerned with something genuinely relevant, but they deceive if they suppose they can grasp Being itself through an immanence which deduces and establishes things. These universal sciences, therefore, can not consolidate themselves. All their demarcations are only relative. Individually, they have the form of cutting across all other sciences. But they never seem to reach their own proper basis, since the encompassing which they have before their eyes is no longer the Encompassing. Their magic is deceptive, but it can become fruitful if there should ensue a sense of the modest, relative, and open character of our knowledge of our own appearance in the world.

Both reason and Existenz have a mode of thinking which awakens them and pushes them toward clarity; to reason belongs philosophical logic, and to Existenz, the clarification of Existenz.

However, if logic pretends to be a universal science of consciousness as such, it loses its philosophical truth and slips into a deceptive science of the Whole. In these magnificent doctrines of categories which unfold themselves out of a single principle, the whole of the Encompassing as the totality of Being itself in its form, the thought of God before creation would be penetrated and reproduced. But these investigations have truth only within an open philosophical logic as an orientation toward the formal possibilities of thought in its many directions which can only be added together, and which are valid for objective appearance; but they are endless and they lack any thoroughly controlling principle which is supposed to produce them. As the elucidation of reason by itself, logic is philosophy and no longer a supposedly objective cognition of the Whole.

The clarification of Existenz does not cognize Existenz, but makes an appeal to its potentialities. However, as "existentialism," it pretends to be discourse about a known object; and precisely because it should perceive its limits and seek to clarify the absolute ground, it only wanders deeper into error, trying to subsume appearances in the world cognitively and judgmentally under its concepts.

Thus the authentic idea of the Encompassing disappears with every attempt to establish, isolate, and absolutize it. An Encompassing which has become objective is no longer the true Encompassing.

The idea of the Encompassing is rather, so to speak, a subverting idea which removes from us all the natural objectivity of our usual thought. In the world, we are concerned with things, contents, objects, but we never question in all this what we have, think, or will. We assert truths, but do not ask what truth itself is. We have to do with questions about the world, but do not ask about the questioner. Dominated by what is important in action or injury, as by something which is attainable and knowable, we never reach the limits from which this whole world of action, possession, and inquiry would become questionable. On the other hand, the idea of the Encompassing requires of us a recognition of the limits of all that exists for us by giving up the usual cognition of objects. Since it sets limits to objective cognition, it frees the real man and all being which he touches from a supposed identity with its knowability, or fixed knownness. Such thinking vitally encompasses the dead being of the known.

This is a simple thought, but philosophically one of infinitely rich consequences. First, it concerns the thinker himself. I am not authentically myself if I am merely what I know myself to be (in all modes of the schemata of the Ego[1] and their determinations). Whenever I objectify myself, I am myself more than this object, namely, I am that being which can thus objectify itself. All characterizations of my being concern me only insofar as I am turned into an object; but, in such an object, I recognize only one side of myself, or myself in one particular aspect, but not myself. If I understand myself exclusively as an empirical existent, as a living natural being, since I have then objectified myself and conceived myself only insofar as I am an object, I have, at the same time, lost myself and substituted what I understand myself to be for what I can be.

To the being of the Encompassing belongs a self-awareness which sees itself just as much as empirical existence and life, as it achieves a critical limiting awareness of itself as consciousness as such and spirit; but it only becomes fully aware of itself, without the impoverishment which comes from absolutizing some limited aspect and the consequent extinction of its potentialities, as reason and Existenz.

Now if I were to soar beyond and conceive myself to be authentic Being itself, i.e., regard myself as Transcendence over and above mere empirical existence, consciousness, or spirit, I should again lose myself in false self-divinization, and cease to be possible Existenz and its actualization.

That *I am* over against all cognizable empirical existence in the world and, at the same time, am posited in my self-created freedom through Transcendence—to affirm such as the position of man in temporal existence is the task on his small path from which he is constantly tempted to deviate, both in his thinking about himself, and in the actual deeds which are connected therewith.

Secondly, the idea concerns absolutely all known being. I know this Other, just as with myself, only as it appears to me and not as it is in itself. No known being is Being itself. Every time I let Being itself slip into known being, Transcendence disappears and I become dark to myself.

In spite of these continual deviations, we must think about the Encompassing in order to make it really present, at first even in a false specificity, but then, by passing through the whole process of these modes of thinking the Encompassing, we can transcend them and push to their source which is no longer an object.

VII. PHILOSOPHICAL RESULT.

The purpose and therefore the meaning of a philosophical idea is not the cognition of an object, but rather an alteration of our consciousness of Being and of our inner attitude toward things.

Understanding the meaning of the Encompassing has the significance of creating a possibility. The philosopher therein says to himself: preserve the open space of the Encompassing! Do not lose yourself in what is merely known! Do not let yourself become separated from Transcendence!

In thinking about temporal existence, one must continually run through the circuit of the modes of the Encompassing. We can remain static in none of its modes. Each demands the others. The loss of one mode lets all the others become false. The philosopher seeks to omit none.

The modes are related to one another. Their tension is not a battle where each seeks to annihilate the others, but rather a mutual enlivening and intensification. Hence the polarity of reason and Existenz must be prevented from being a mutual exclusion; rather, instead of each turning away from the other in hostility, each should grow through mutual questioning.

The relation between the two is not that of flat reciprocity but goes up and down. One can not expect that the higher will be automatically produced by the lower, or that with the lower as a condition, the higher can be depended upon to arise. For the higher has its own proper cause. The higher gives limits and order of rank to the lower without being able, however, to generate it. One should never forget the relation of every mode of the Encompassing to every other and the direction of this relation.

So far, every mode of the Encompassing appears in the light of reason as something relatively dark, and thus there is an external similarity among them in terms of more or less reason. An awareness of this requires that the philosopher not substitute mere vitality for Existenz, or Nature for Transcendence.

The open space of such philosophizing becomes a danger unless one keeps in steady consciousness one's potential Existenz: there is a danger that one may see oneself as lost through abstract thinking on the whole range of things. Genuine thinking about the Encompassing, however, is reflected back from the total range of revealed directions ever so much more decisively onto the concrete historicity of my own present. Now for the first time it is possible to be in the present without disappearing into the restrictions of the unthinking, the blind, and the unrelated. Now also it is possible to grasp the whole spaciousness of Being without losing oneself in the void of the mere universal of the understanding, in the meaningless facticity of empirical existence, or in some empty beyond. For the determinateness of the historical depths is bound up with the openness of unlimited ranges of Being, and the truth of one's own bases with their relation to the ungrounded openness of Being, Existenz with reason. The more unrestrictedly I penetrate by thought into the depths, the truer my love becomes in its historical present. Hölderlin said: "Who has thought about the deepest, loves what is most alive."

Man can seek the path of his truth in unfanatical absoluteness, in a decisiveness which remains open.

third lecture

TRUTH AS COMMUNICABILITY

INTRODUCTION: FROM THE AMPLITUDE OF THE ENCOMPASSING TO THE BOND THROUGH COMMUNICATION.

The question of truth can be posed in its greatest amplitude through the knowledge of the modes of the Encompassing which we have discussed in the last lecture. In each of these modes Being and truth have a proper and distinct sense. We only grasp truth if we experience it in every horizon and omit none of its modes.

But in each of these modes there occurs a retraction from the vastness of the Encompassing, which as mere vastness would tend to sink into nothingness, through that binding which grows out of what is common to all truth in all modes of the Encompassing: that to be genuinely true, truth must be communicable.

We represent this original phenomenon of our humanity thus: we are what we are only through the community of mutually conscious understandings. There can be no man who is a man for himself alone, as a mere individual.

A. Comparison of man with animal.

Animals either are what they are as individuals, in all their generations always the same through heredity and natural growth; or they build communities into which they are unconsciously absorbed through their instincts, bringing forth repeatable, identical, non-historical structures according to strict natural law; they are indifferently replaceable functions of the whole. Thus animals on the one hand pass into the immediate actuality of a community which is tightly held together, or on the other hand they run independently of one another as if nothing had happened—natural processes always dominated by the moment's instinct. Animals make themselves understood instinctively. That they find themselves together, give something like signs to one another, even, as individuals, bind themselves fast to one another does not mean that they are bound together in a human bond in which men, to some degree, express themselves. With animals it is always a consequence of an unconscious and, in its meaning to men, inaccessible biological order, always in an unhistorical identity with simply other examples.

Man, on the other hand, is comparatively more detached as an individual than many animals, but his community also conditions him more decisively, and this community is essentially different from that of the animals.

The human community in analogy to the animal is weak from the point of view of supplying a natural and reliable bond. Purely biologically, man here, as everywhere, is below the animals. His community is, first of all, no state of immediacy, but is mediated through a relation to something else: through a relation to common conscious purposes in the world, through a relation to truth, and through relation to God.

Secondly, human communication is continually moved in its relation to these changing potential contents; it finds no resting place and, unlike that of the animals, has no repeating final goal. It is historical and on a path of unceasing change of which the beginning and end are not visible, a change through the recollection and appropriation of the past as well as through ever new planning for a future. Human communities, therefore, stand in opposition to those of the animals in their potentiality for an incalculable continuity in unfolding and gathering together out of the past and present. Thus, through this movement, it is a continually insecure and endangered reality which must always re-establish itself, limit and expand itself, test itself, and push on. In its true being it does not possess its final state, but rather is only directed toward it. It exists therefore in the tension of detours, errors, somersaults, and recoveries.

Thirdly, because of this manner of movement, human nature is not solely a matter of heredity, but also of tradition. Every new human being begins in communication, and not merely with his biological nature. This is externally visible in the unfortunate cases of deaf mutes in the past, who, in consequence of an inborn or early acquired deafness (and lacking modern education which today brings them to complete humanity), remained undeveloped; since they could not hear it, speech was without influence upon them, and thus they could not participate in tradition. They were hardly distinguishable from real idiots.

This comparison of man and animal only points to communication as the universal condition of man's being. It is so much his comprehensive essence that both what man is and what is for him are in some sense bound up with communication. The Encompassing which we are is, in every form, communication; the Encompassing which is Being itself exists for us only insofar as it achieves communicability by becomng speech or becoming utterable.

B. Truth in Communication.

Truth therefore cannot be separated from communicability. It only appears in time as a reality-through-communication. Abstracted from communication, truth hardens into an unreality. The movement of communication is at one and the same time the preservation of, and the search for, the truth.

In general then, it applies to my being, my authenticity, and my grasp of the truth that, not only factually am I not for myself alone, but I can not even become myself alone without emerging out of my being with others.

I. A. Communication in the Encompassing which we are: communication in empirical existence, in consciousness as such, and in spirit.

Truth is not of one sort, single and unique in its meaning. It has as many senses as there are modes of communication in which it arises. For what truth is, is determined by the character of the Encompassing within which communication takes place; for example, communication from one empirical existent to another, or in consciousness as such, or in the idea of spirit; and then further, it is determined by whether it is achieved in the binding together of these modes of the Encompassing in reason, and its basis, Existenz. The truth which is ever valid is determined by the Encompassing in which we stand in communication, by who communicates, and by whom the communication is understood.

We shall analyze the modes of the Encompassing by inquiring into the kind of communication which occurs in them, characterizing them singly as though they were separable.

1. The Encompassing of our mere empirical existence is not identical with our empirical existence as already scientifically known; rather it remains as a problem for advancing knowledge through all our acquired knowledge of its physiological, psychological, and sociological character.

This empirical existence of ours has the will to preserve and develop itself without limits; it wills satisfaction and happiness. To achieve these goals, the Encompassing of empirical existence demands the communication of a community which can preserve life. Interest (or rather what each holds to be his interest) is again found in the other. Need binds them all together against nature, which threatens all in common, and against other communities. The private interests of each individual existent at the same time stand in tension toward this bond, almost always ready to break out of the community when there is any slackening of the need. According to Kant, "unsocial sociability," in which none can dispense with yet none tolerate the other, is the basic feature of empirical existence. Communication on this level of empirical existence can be characterized as follows:

Danger forces everyone quickly and easily to comprehend what is necessary. But how this is understood is based upon the experience of the majority, the average, that which when it is said is understood by everybody. The similarity within the species defines what happiness or satisfaction is, what is necessary for life.

Further, on this level of communication, the greater the danger, the more decisively is the unity of the will of all necessary. And this is only to be secured through obedience. Hence not every individual can decide what it is necessary to do to fulfill the interests in sheer existence.

How this is to occur gives rise to the many forms of government. In the communication of the community, we do not find a simple relation between a single omniscient commander and the masses of everybody else who unthinkingly obey; rather there are always many together in a complex organization who in mutual understanding work out their decision.

In the empirical community, therefore, insofar as we isolate it in its meaning, it is the pragmatic concept of truth which is valid: truth does not lie in something already known, or something finally knowable, or in an absolute, but rather in what arises and comes to pass. Here there is only a relative and changing truth, for empirical existence itself changes. This process can run so that my opponent's standpoint which for me today is wrong, tomorrow, in a changed situation, may be relevant to my purposes. Constructive acts in the community are perpetual compromises. Compromise is the truth which does not forget that every standpoint, no matter how right it seems, can also be refuted through the very fact of process. Accordingly, for the continuity of a living community the art of conversation must be developed.[1]

2. The communication of consciousness as such [*Bewusstsein überhaupt*] is that between point-consciousnesses, indifferently replaceable, dissimilar yet agreeing, which, through the dichotomies of the knowable (subject-object, form-matter, anything and its other), by means of all the logical categories, grasp in affirmation and denial that which is valid for everybody. It is the communication of a self-identical consciousness dispersed into the multiplicities of its empirical existence. The communication occurs in a disinterested attention upon some matter one is inquiring into, either into its factual character or into its validity through agreed-upon methods of argument.

3. The communication of spirit is the emergence of the Idea of a whole out of the communal substance. The individual is conscious of standing in a place which has its proper meaning only in that whole. His communication is that of a member with its organism. He is different, as all the others are, but agrees with them in the order which comprehends all. They communicate with one another out of the common presence of the Idea. In this communication, it is as though some whole not clearly knowable by consciousness as such spoke, limited itself, and gave indications of whence it came. When the communication is not enlivened with the actual content of this whole, to that extent it slips into the indifferent and trivial.

B. Comparison of meanings of truth.

In each of these three modes of the Encompassing which we are—empirical existence, consciousness as such, and spirit—there is always an appropriate sense of truth. Truth for empirical existence comes from usefulness of consequences for action, and from custom. It is a function of self-preserving and developing existence. Here truth is not based upon its own independent grounds, but arises out of action and exists for action in a mobility of generation and preservation which ultimately is purposeless. In the medium of consciousness as such, truth is a cogent correctness. As pure understanding, everyone insofar as he understands at all must see this correctness. The evidence pertains to the understanding itself as a function of its grasp of the timeless rightness of what is universally valid. In the medium of spirit, it is conviction which counts, a conviction which is confirmed out of the Idea. Out of the substance of a whole, I recognize as true from my place in the community of the whole that which belongs to an historical totality.

Intended pragmatic endurance, cogent evidence, and full conviction are the three senses of truth in these three forms of the Encompassing. A further comparison of communication in the three modes will be concerned with the nature of him who communicates, and who he is. For, in fact, we are not always identical on every level of meaning in our speaking. In the multiplicity of speeches and assertions, which so often are no longer understood, the question: who speaks? is clarifying.

If it is empirical existence that speaks, it is not a question of truth in all earnestness, but rather, whether hidden or clear, of what appears to this empirical existence as relevant to his interests and desires, of what he seeks to satisfy him in the world of the senses, of wealth, power, or whatever other form the inevitably ambiguous "happiness" appears to him.

If consciousness as such speaks, then an absolutely universal, possible understanding must occur in both speech and reply for the speaking to be meaningful. A meaningful argument therefore requires that the words describe something definite, that they not be equivocal, and the recognition that the contradictory cancels itself. It is therefore impossible to have a discussion which aims at something universally valid with someone who does not regard the identity of consciousness as such as the speaker. Such a one is entangled in the empirical existence of a living being, "almost like the plants" (Aristotle), and is to be regarded either as such, or as a vital will which is concealing itself. But when consciousness as such speaks, it is, in that respect, like an empty, indifferently replaceable point.

For communication of spirit to be possible, it is not sufficient that I as a pure understanding recognize and follow the principles of identity and contradiction. Who speaks and understands here speaks out of the substance of an Idea. He must be filled with something which is not merely an object in the world which could be known by consciousness as such. Only out of this new source can the meaning of what is said be grasped and developed.

If we call a community which understands itself a "community of minds," then such a community has a threefold sense:

Empirically, it is a community of vital sympathies and interests; it is continually mobile, always delimiting itself against others, expanding, and then again breaking up into smaller parts.

On the level of consciousness as such, it is the universality of the general, that which binds all men together identically as understandings in an impersonal community which has no actual power and which is determined by the merely valid.

As a community of the spirit, the members are united through the knowledge of a whole into the community of its Idea. It is always *a* whole, never *the* whole, and it must as a whole relate itself to other wholes and always remain uncompleted in its own actual existence.

II. A. The will to communicate of reason and Existenz; unsatisfactoriness of the three modes of communication.

The representation of the human community in these three modes of the Encompassing does not yet show what truth really is, even though truth plays a role in each of the moments we have touched upon. And it has not yet shown the final ground and basis for the possibility of communication.

Community through communication is found, to be sure, already among the merely living existences; it is in consciousness as such, and it is in spirit. However, on the level of mere vitality, it can remain instinctive sympathies or interests limited to certain purposes. In consciousness as such, it can remain an unconcerned agreement upon what is correct or valid; in spirit, a deceptive consciousness of totality which however suddenly breaks off fellowship.

There is an insufficiency in every mode of the Encompassing, an insufficiency as much in communication as in truth. This insufficiency can be made intelligible initially by pointing out the limits which show that no mode of the Encompassing can stand by itself:

Mere empirical existence seeks gratification, survival, happiness. Its limit however is that the nature of happiness remains both unclear and questionable. A man whose every wish was fulfilled would be destroyed in consequence. No happiness is permanent, and every fulfillment is deceptive. The meaninglessness of the will which is forever desiring yet which has no goal is an old theme in philosophy.

Consciousness as such touches on the universally valid

truth. But its limit is that these indubitable validities as such are trivialities, and they can be heaped up in a senseless infinity.

Spirit grasps the Idea of the whole. Its limit however is that which can not be absorbed into spirit, the reality of the less-than-total, of the contingent, of the merely factual.

If one level of the Encompassing is absolutized, we must always question those characteristic phenomena which appear when the other modes of the Encompassing are neglected and the limits of this one ignored.

1. What happens when natural existence as such is not only regarded as Being itself but also when one so acts? What happens, in other words, when such a naturalistic idea is not only uttered, but when the idea is practiced, when the absolutizing of the level of empirical existence is accomplished in fact?

When this happens there occurs a surrender of both the universally valid truth of consciousness in general and the Ideas of the spirit. To be sure, in the beginning there still can be present a certain honesty which grasps the deceptiveness of merely intellectual thinking detached from reality, of a detached and merely cultured spirit. In fact, many times a passionate "idealism" which strives for Substance can be found working in a new "materialism." But afterwards, through the influence of the contents of the thought insofar as their consequences are actually drawn, the meaning of the hidden source of truth becomes lost, a meaning which was still present as a negative truthfulness in a self-deceived will to authentic being. Then it might happen that, recklessly following the contingencies and laws of empirical existence, I would will nothing else, I would renounce communication on the level of valid and intelligible truth or effective Ideas in general. Or perhaps I would merely savor them as attitudes or charming efforts in realms irrelevant to and unaffected by the conflict of existence where force and cleverness rule, attitudes which have no real influence upon the will to know or communicate. Thus conceived they are fraudulent experiences.

The confidence in nature, whose origin is a metaphysical confidence in the grounds of Being, is changed into a confidence in those insufficient, known, yet always questionable, regularities which scientific investigation wrings out of appearance. The essence of man is lost in this blind reliance upon nature, where his existence seems identical with nature, and nature identical with knowable regularities. For even if those regularities or laws were exhaustively known, they would only make matter and biological life comprehensible, not man—only man as a species of animal, which could then be called the endangered, the sick animal. When human consciousness becomes the only possibility in the known world, man loses himself in the simple affirmation of his impulses which, however, he can not let work with animal naturalness or unquestioned simplicity of meaning. Thus, in the helpless confusion of his empirical existence which ensues, his thought and spiritual possibilities vanish into a thoughtless obedience to incomprehensible forces above or in him, simply in order to exist here and now.

If we extrapolate such a tendency to its limit in a distant future, it would be possible for man to relapse into an animal-like existence which preserved a technical apparatus like ants, but an apparatus which arose in another mental world and remained as a residue. It would be only a self-repeating, non-historical species of living thing, the result of an astonishing, but now forgotten, intermediary moment of humanity. What was once incorporated and proven in the struggle for existence to be useful for the preservation and expansion of existence would now have become instinct. In all the chaos of natural existence, it could last a long time like other forms of life until, with a thorough change in the living conditions on the surface of the earth, final catastrophe would also come to this species.

2. When the thinking of consciousness as such circles

around in self-sufficiency, then it is taking its timeless validities as absolute, as though the truth and Being itself were thereby grasped, as though it had read off the order and laws of things beyond all relativity. Through the abstraction of the thinking consciousness from Being, responsibility ceases for the being which is living being and spirit. The empty play of a dissolving intellectualism begins, a play which in fact is actually directed by psychologically knowable impulses.

3. The absolutizing of spirit in a wealth of merely understood contents is simply an intensified mode of the isolation of thinking. In its self-satisfaction it creates a hollow world of culture under contingent, favorable conditions, an object of pleasure, of unreal longing, a realm of flight and negativity.

What is unsatisfactory in the communication of the true in all these hitherto mentioned modes of the Encompassing could lie in the isolation of single modes. From this standpoint, true communication is already under the following demands: none of the modes can be ignored; to play off one against the other is to miss the ground of their connection. For true communication it is important to perceive the limits of every level and therewith their inability to be completed in themselves, and further, not to deceive oneself by a fixation on one of the levels over the possibility of a communication which goes through all.

The binding together of the modes of the Encompassing is here in the form of a rising series where the succeeding can be real only under the conditions set by the preceding. The termination of the preceding in isolation against the succeeding always means a specific break-off of communication. Thus a two-fold formal requirement is laid upon communication: 1) The lower level is to be limited so that it is conditioned by the possibility of the higher. For example, communication on the level of mere existence must be under the condition that evident truth remains valid and under the Ideas of spirit. 2) The higher level can not be actualized for itself in isolation, but only under the presuppositions of the lower which it delimits and breaks through but to which it must hold fast. Thus the will to knowledge must not forget its incorporation as science in the community of human beings, nor must the spirit forget its entire dependence upon empirical existence if they are not forthwith to disappear.

The higher levels are made possible by the effects of the lower and, perhaps, influenced by them. The lower on the other hand are given direction by the higher in always determinate ways.

In empirical existence the higher levels are the weaker. For the lower levels can stand without the higher, not in their authentic truth, but still as sheer existents. From this two consequences follow: First, there is something like guilt toward empirical existence when I blindly rely upon univocal obligations of higher levels of the Encompassing without considering their relation to empirical existence, letting these higher obligations themselves be destroyed by more powerful existences. Thus Max Weber in the political sphere opposed an ethics of principle which would let itself be pushed to destruction through adherence to some single law (acting unconditionally according to moral axioms and justifying itself by having willed the good and trusting in God for the result). He argued instead for an ethics of responsibility where one is concerned also for the consequences (even though the formulations of such an ethics can be misused arbitrarily). I let myself and my friends be pushed into the position of the weaker, the impotent, the ruined, by holding to attitudes which may be valid on their own level; but, where I am not acting on this level, I simply am misused and abandoned to the cleverness of others.

Secondly, endless duration of empirical existence as such

can not be a meaningful goal. Man can endure as a sheer existent, but he ceases thereby to be man, just as every living being can die, and dead matter have the victorious duration. The lower in rank, the greater the durability of a being. The higher levels are the more mobile, more imperiled, more perishable. The will to endure in time, except through the limited continuity of a changing and fulfilling historicity, is a misunderstanding of the meaning of these higher levels.

Thus everywhere we see how the absolutization and isolation of one mode of the Encompassing shows its limits and at the same time the falseness which arises therewith. The unsatisfied will to communicate can be satisfied only according to the formula: every mode of communicability has its right, none can be omitted. It would always be a fault in the realization of my will to communicate if I were to ignore any level as unimportant.

Further, since the modes of the Encompassing are not separate things which can be set alongside one another and which together as a sum make up what I am as a whole, it is inadequate to present them as alternatives for some supposed choice. Rather it is necessary to apprehend them in their order of rank.

But this whole way of looking at things still leaves something in us unsatisfied. It is as though the essential had not yet been said. What is decisively unsatisfactory can be felt first of all in this: that the modes of the Encompassing in no way lead to the unity of a self-completed whole. Neither can the essential differences in the meaning of communication and truth in the three modes be effaced; nor can they be reduced to a knowable totality. It would be a deception to suppose that the modes of the Encompassing and the kinds of communication could grow into one another so that a harmonious whole would be possible in temporal existence.

Secondly, this dissatisfaction of ours, that first strove to grasp all the modes of communication together and then experienced its impossibility, sprang out of an impulse which, in its unlimited dissatisfaction and its open readiness for all sides, itself belongs to none of the three modes of the Encompassing. Even the will to communicate in these three modes holds its own energy at the service of a universal will to communicate which comes out of reason and Existenz. Let us now characterize this further.[2]

B. Existential and rational communication.

If even the basic problem for empirical existents, which can endure only through community, is how one is to understand the other, how we can think and will the same things so that we can be actively bound together, then the authentic human essence, Existenz and reason, can nowhere be touched as deeply as by the question of its communication.

The communication of Existenz is accomplished through membership in the spirit, through the universality of consciousness as such, through proving itself in empirical existence, but also by breaking through these, passing beyond them in the loving struggle of those who will to become themselves. In contrast to the communication of identical and indifferently replaceable points of consciousness as such, this existential communication is between irreplaceable individuals. In contrast to the struggle for existence over power, superiority, and annihilation, here the struggle over the content of Existenz is without the will to power in the same sense; it is a struggle where every advance of the individual comes only if the other advances too, and every destruction of the other is my own. In contrast to spiritual community, where there is security in the comprehensive Idea, it does not overlook the crack in Being for us, and it is open for Transcendence. It expresses the inevitability of struggle in temporal existence and the inability of truth to be completed by unceasingly pushing the movement of communication forward as the authentic appearance of truth. To be self and to be true are nothing else than to be in communication unconditionally. Here in the depths, to preserve oneself would be precisely to lose oneself.

Existenz, then, only becomes apparent and thereby real if it comes to itself through, and at the same time with, another Existenz. What is authentically human in the community of reason and Existenz is not, as before in physical life, simply present in a plurality of naturally generated examples, which then find one another and bind themselves together. Rather communication seems to produce for the first time that which is communicating: independent natures which come to consciousness of themselves, however, as though they were not touched by the contingencies of empirical existence, but had been bound together eternally.

Since this occurs in historical situations which are always new, every form of Existenz which unfolds itself in communication is both the revelation of an irreplaceable (because historical) and essentially never repeatable selfhood, and also an unconditional binding together of historical men.

Now, in existential communication, reason is what penetrates everything. Existenz as the ground bears in its depths the organ which is present in all modes of the Encompassing, which is the universal bond as well as the unrest which disturbs every fixation. Reason, having its substance in Existenz, arises from the authentic communication of one nature with another, and it arises in such a fashion that empirical existence, consciousness as such, and spirit are, so to speak, the body of its appearance. Not for an instant is reason without these, and they are all moved and changed by it.

Reason is potential Existenz which in its thinking is continually directed upon an other, upon the Being which we are not, upon the world, and upon Transcendence. What these are then becomes communicable and, therewith, being-for-us, but in the formality through which they authentically touch Existenz. Reason is present as an unlimited drive in empirical existence, in consciousness as such, and in the spirit. No range is sufficient for it; as a passionate will-to-know oriented toward the world, it reaches no end. How Existenz is shipwrecked upon Transcendence becomes clear through reason. Reason moves toward rendering all Being transparent to itself only to experience the shock of the absolutely opaque, which as such is accessible only to the clearest reason. The content of the other made present by reason is at the same time the measure of the depths of the communication which is possible, and of the character of men who are altered therein and unfold in rank in innumerable ways.

The higher sense of the word reason should be preserved. It should not sink to mean mere comprehensiblity, spirituality, or the necessities of empirical existence. Its sense however can not be immediately expressed or pointed out in a fixed definition but only through the movement of a philosophical logic.

Communication remains original and unrestricted only where reason is dependably present, a reason which as a source can not be objectified nor directly perceived in any argumentation. It is truth itself, the total will-to-communicate.

That man always holds himself still in reserve, or, so to speak, hovers over what he knows, does, is, somewhere has its limits if he is not nothing, or if he is not merely the formal empty point of this hovering. The limits are there where he is; he is himself as reason, and he is reason as potential Existenz. But, as a consequence, reason and Existenz can not be objectified like the modes of the Encompassing. Where thought transcends to reason and Existenz, nothing is reached except the inner perception of the possibility of this unknowable selfhood, which is only as the communication of Existenz through reason.

The way in which reason and Existenz belong together is not, however, that of mere identity. If Existenz finds the limit of what is counter-rational in every sense, which coincides with the break-off of all communication, still, it can perceive this possibility in itself only through reason. This negative Existenz, to which no thought and being can follow, remains true—that is, does not collapse into the restrictions of a definite mode of the Encompassing, but remains as something lost and without a world before an incomprehensible Transcendence—only by a path which leads above the full realization of the reason which it has finally surrendered.[3]

C. Resumé of meanings of truth.

If Existenz and reason are, so to speak, the ground and bond of the three modes of the Encompassing which we are, we now can summarize our comparisons of the senses of truth in these three modes:

1. We distinguish among the senses of truth pragmatic preservation of empirical existence, cogent evidence for consciousness as such, and conviction in the spiritual Idea. As Existenz, I experience truth in faith whose truth however is not yet comprised in those three. Where there is no effective preservation of existence, no demonstrable certitude, no longer any saving wholeness, there I come upon a depth of truth where, without leaving that whole which is my actual world, I break through it in order to return to it out of the experience of Transcendence, at one and the same time in and out of it.

2. We distinguish in these meanings of truth who it is that speaks in communicating the truth. In existential and rational communication, it is the existing man who speaks decisively—the man who is not merely living vitality, nor merely an abstract understanding, but who is himself in all of these.

3. We distinguish modes in the community of mind. Existenz finds itself in a realm of mind which can not be closed, of Existenz open before Transcendence. Out of

such a realm, the forms of community which develop in the modes of the Encompassing first derive their soul, while these forms always remain the indispensable appearance, the condition for the actualization of Existenz—a condition which must be both participated in and broken through.

III. A. The meaning of truth and the will to total communication.

The dissatisfaction with every particular mode of communication leads to a will to total communication, a will which can only be one and which is the authentically driving and binding force in all the modes of communication.

But this will to communicate, which actualizes itself out of potential Existenz through reason in the three modes of the Encompassing, itself does not reach fulfillment. For it is continuously bound within the three modes, and, although aroused and moved, yet it is, so to speak, muddied in its mode. And, finally, it finds itself limited through its own, as well as through others', historicity. This historicity both brings communication in its depths before the multiplicity of truth and also lets it be wrecked.

From this situation of Existenz in time, it follows first that, if truth is bound up with communication, truth itself can only *become*—that, in its depths, it is not dogmatic but communicative. Out of the consciousness of a becoming truth, first springs the possibility of a radical openness of the will to communicate in actuality—a will, however, that can never fulfill itself except in an historical moment which, precisely as such, becomes incommunicable.

There follows secondly, in being wrecked by the multiplicity of truth, a self-recovery of the unlimited will to communicate in an attitude which just as resolutely envisages failure in the whole while it nevertheless holds to its path, not knowing where it leads.

It follows thirdly that, if truth in communication can never be definitively won and established—truth like communication seeing itself, so to speak, disappear before Transcendence, change before Being—nevertheless, its resolute actualization brings forth also the deepest openness for Transcendence.

B. The double sense of truth in time (dogmatic and communicative truth).

The question is, how far total communication is the reality of truth, our truth in time. The question will become clear by distinguishing two senses of truth in time:

When truth seemed to be grasped historically and conclusively in object, symbol, and expression, then the question still remained how such a truth, attained and now present, was to be transmitted to all men. Such truth was closed in itself, timeless in time, and therefore complete to itself and independent of men. But men had their value dependent upon it. Communication from man to man then began which was not a cooperative production, but rather a giving of a possessed truth, to which they referred, but in which they did not participate. And therewith began the process by which this truth changed. For they took it in, understood it in itself, but in fact there was no surrender to it. The truth, instead of being given to men while it itself remained in its original purity, was watered down and perverted, or, in the transformation, became something totally different out of new origins. Its spread among men in such forms went to the limits beyond which its further spread was factually impaired.

The truth which from the first would bind itself to communication would be different. It would not be found outside of its incorporation in communication. In itself, it would neither be nor be complete. As conditions, it would have changes, not only in the men to whom it would be communicated, but also in the men who would communicate, in consequence of their readiness and ability to communicate—their resolute capacities for speaking and hearing and their inward perception of all modes and levels of communication. It would be a truth which would arise for the first time in communication, which would become actual only in and through it; it would be a truth which is neither already here to be transmitted to another, nor which presents us with a methodically attainable end in which it could be valid without communication.

Historically, permanent truths have been developed into philosophical and religious techniques for the formation of men. All those *exercitia spiritualia,* yoga exercises, and mystic initiations have sought to transform the individual into a perception of the truth, not by communication, but by a self-sufficient discipline. But if one will not remain satisfied with such fixed, leveling, final, and therefore degenerative types of man as his supposed fulfillment, even though they may have their own magnificence, he will need a deeper discipline of a communication continually exercised with perspicuity. That which was often reached by restriction to rationally clear ends but which beyond that accomplished little in historical communities and that little always questionable—that must be the beginning: what is required is the bringing forth of humanity under the conditions of a communication which is not deceptive, not superficial, not degenerating, but limitlessly clarifying.

But, even in this communication, falsehood must also be present insofar as truth, in its movement, is never complete, but in every factual completion also remains continuously open.

Again, there is a radical abyss between the dogmatic and the communicative modes of knowing the truth:

If the presupposition is made of a permanent truth which as such is accessible to us, and if it is valid as something fixed outside of me that is already there needing only to be found, then our problem is simply to discover it, and not to produce it. Then, either there would be a single world-order of a purely immanent sort and our problem would be to set it up, or there would be a Beyond which is only like another world in safer prospect.

If, however, truth for us in every form remains a limit in the realization of communication, then the insurmountable incompleteness of the world and all worldly, knowable truth is final for immanence. Every form of truth must be shipwrecked in the world, and none can substitute itself absolutely for the truth.

If, therefore, there is truth in this last way, then it can only be in the Transcendence which is not some Beyond as a mere second world, or this world taken again as a better world. The idea which grasps Transcendence from the unfulfillment of all communication and from the shipwrecking of every form of truth in the world is like a proof of God: from the unfulfillment of every sense of truth and under the assumption that truth must be, thought touches upon Transcendence. Such an idea is valid only for Existenz which is an absolute concern for truth, and to whose honesty truth, as a single, unique, and static possession of timelessness, never shows itself in the world.

C. The openness of the will-to-communicate on its path through existence.

Philosophically, to become conscious of communicative truth comes to this: so to think through all the modes of the Encompassing that potential Existenz has the largest space in the world. Existenz, as irremediably a movement in time, should hold itself open before the whole range of possibilities and actualities. Only then can that radical will-to-communicate which springs out of reason and Existenz work; whereas the possession of truth as though it were conclusively asserted in fact breaks communication off.

The openness in the will-to-communicate is a double one: first, openness to the knowability of what is not yet known. Since that which is not communicable is as though it were not at all, openness strives to bring every possibility into the medium of communication so that it might attain being for us. Secondly, this openness must be ready to encounter the substance of every being that really communicates with me as another who I am not, but in solidarity with whom I can without limit will to become myself. This loving search of men reaches no termination.

My consciousness however remains continually restricted: in the first place, by that being which, lacking communicability, is not for me but which, unnoticed by me, works upon my existence and my world; and, in the second place, by the empirical existence and Existenz of others who are not identical with me and do not think in the same way, but who through their communication also determine my empirical existence without my knowing it, and whose communication can bring me still closer to myself. Hence my consciousness is never the absolutely true consciousness for it is never the whole. Through this unexpected effect, I am continually reminded not to stop in the movement toward truth; otherwise my own truth will discover that matters themselves have gone beyond me. Truth, said Hegel, is in league with reality against consciousness. This reality is given in the workings of what is not communicated, and perhaps is incommunicable, in the world, as that which we hear without understanding what comes between us, and as what we can only suffer. The unlimited will-to-communicate, then, never means simply to submit oneself to the other as such, but rather to know that other, to hear him, to will to reckon with him even unto the necessity of a transformation of oneself.

Living in the totality of the Encompassing in which I find myself is therefore necessarily a venture. Clarification itself shows me in a situation of venture, not because I seek danger out of bravado, but because I must venture. Only a life which remains blind can mask from itself this standing risk and remain between the polarity of supposed safety and a rising, but then immediately forgotten, anxiety. It is risk to see the possible pushed to its highest degree, to dare to entice it out at the risk of one's own openness and bearing responsibility for which men I trust and how I trust myself—and knowing that on every level communication is only possible among equals. I must assume responsibility for failure and deception, perhaps as a crisis in which communication can for the first time grow, perhaps as a disaster which I can not understand.

D. The many-fold existential truth for the radical will-to-communicate.

Where the Encompassing remains present in every form, the will-to-communicate can be genuinely total; and there Existenz stands before its final limits: that there are many truths in the sense of existential absolutes.

To recognize philosophically this multiplicity of truths can seem fickle. One can object: only a single truth is the truth absolutely, if not for God at least for man; man can not act categorically if he does not believe his truth to be the only one.

To this there is a reply. Since it is impossible for man to have Transcendence in time as a knowable object, identical for everybody like something in the world, every mode of the One Truth as absolute in the world can in fact only be historical: unconditional for this Existenz but, precisely for this reason, not universally valid. For, since it is not impossible, but only psychologically infinitely difficult, for a man to act according to his own truth, realizing at the same time the truth of others which is not truth for him, holding fast to the relativity and particularity of all universally valid truths—since it is not impossible, he must not shirk this highest demand of truthfulness which is only apparently incompatible with that of others. The Idea of man can not be projected too high so long as the absolutely impossible is avoided, that which contradicts his finitude in time. The empirically improbable, i.e., that which is improbable in the light of the actual, average, observable human species, is not valid before the Idea of a communication ready for anything, which is possible in the basis of human nature. Before the empirical reality such an Idea changes itself into an unending problem whose limits of accomplishment are not foreseeable.

The most radical disruption of communication lies close to the existential recognition of the plurality of truths. Yet the total will-to-communicate, once it is on its way, can not surrender itself. It has a confidence in itself and in possibilities in the world which may be deceived again and again, but it can doubt only its limited expressions, never its own principle. It trusts the truth of others which is not its own, but which, as truth, must contain a possibility of communication. Thus it can not collapse absolutely under the burden of failure. Perhaps a courageous modesty suits it best, where it projects a vision of its path as an Idea, to be sure without any extensive reality, but as an expression of a possibility which never betrays itself.

For example, the greatest extremes of clarity and truth can still enter into warring enmity if, in the struggle for existence, fundamentally and essentially different Existenzen apprehend unavoidably diverse destinies. Out of their potential communication, they may put the struggle under rules, thereby ceasing to be concealed beasts, and fight chivalrously, that is, under laws which presuppose potential Existenz on both sides, and which do not make genuine future communication impossible. Yet, if this were attained, the leap to genuine communication would already in fact have been accomplished; the struggle would be subordinated to conditions, no longer a course of events flowing from the necessities of empirical existence, but rather like a play, even though a play which is portentous, life-imperiling, and perhaps life-destroying.

Only thus would an unlimited will-to-communicate be honestly maintained. A humanity might arise which would not be weak, but rather capable of unforeseeable growth through openness, touched by every real Substance, a unique consciousness of limits where the reality of action points, not to some dogmatically hardened, but rather to a genuine Transcendence.

Only thus can the genuine strength of man be developed. The power of the absolute in man tested in every possibility of struggle and questioning no longer needs the power of suasion, hatred, and cruelty in order to become active; nor the intoxication of magniloquent words and unintelligible dogmas in order to be believed in. And in such ways it would only become rough, harsh, and disillusioned. Only thus can self-deception disappear without man also being destroyed through the destruction of his vital lies. Only thus does the genuine Ground reveal itself unmasked out of the depths.

On the other hand, falseness sets in with the assertion of a single truth as valid for all men, despite the greatness of the men who lived thereby and the greatness of their history.

This is shown by the most manifold connections. If this one truth in the form of an intuitive, universal validity is taken as the form of all truth and for the work of reason, or inversely as a super-rational or counter-rational matter of faith, then everyone must bow before such a mighty truth without thereby being able to be himself. Thus, as a consequence of the false presupposition of a unique form of truth accessible to man, and as a consequence of what is connected therewith—the perversion of the multiplicity of the Encompassing—an incomprehension continually arises at the limits of what does not agree with one's own truth. Then suddenly a fanaticism appears which disrupts all communication. In the apparently free medium of speech, communication, listening, showing, and the giving of reasons, secretly the brutal force of what is momentarily the most powerful in existence is deciding.

However, a doctrine of the plurality of truths would

have the same effect in producing falseness, if it appeared as a dogma of the deplorable multiplicity of truths instead of being an attitude of unlimited willingness to communicate one's own possible truth. The plurality of truths is untrue at the moment when they are seen externally as many, as determinable standpoints; for every standpoint can also absorb him who thinks it. They become even more untrue when they become mutually indifferent and simply rest alongside one another. What will not and what can not become the same, nevertheless, become related through Transcendence which touches the One, which, even if our gods be different, beyond all closer gods, discovers the distant God, which requires of us not to relapse into the distraction of warring multiplicities related only by indifference or the struggle over room to exist. There is the sophistry of an easy tolerance which wishes to be valid, but not to be really touched. On the other hand, there is the truth of tolerance which listens and gives and enters into the unpredictable process of communication by which force is restrained; in such a process, man reaches from his roots to the heights possible for him. The very highest arrives only through a transforming appropriation, through a knowledge which, even though it repudiates itself, searches into everything which can be encountered in the world.

To demand fulfillment and salvation in time, or even the picture of salvation, would be to cancel the problem of men, who must always become themselves through communication. It comes to this: never close off authentic possibilities of human development by anticipation.

Our horizon is not closed off with the contents of completed pictures. What is final for us philosophically is the forms of our attitude, sketches of a project which itself is to be thought of only as form, truths which are experienced only in their tendency, not alien impossibilities, but rather possibilities which are just beginning to speak even when they also appear to sink away again.

E. Transcendence: appearance of temporal existence as communication.

The unfulfillment of communication and the difficulty of bearing its shipwreck become the revelation of a depth which nothing other than Transcendence can fill. If God is eternal, still for man truth is as a developing truth, indeed, a truth developing in communication. Abstracted from this as something permanent, truth instead of remaining itself degenerates into determinate knowledge, into a finished contentment instead of a demand that consumes temporal existence.

Before Transcendence, however, the unfulfillment of communication disappears as the temporal appearance of truth. Our communication is, so to speak, animated by something which is expressed in the play of some metaphysical ideas: a pretemporal origin of a temporal need to communicate, or a final fulfillment which surpasses communication. Such ideas can not make anything clearly knowable, but in their collapse they can touch for a moment the overwhelming impulse which is the actual power in genuine communication.

In the beginning was the One, the Truth as it is inaccessible to us. But it is as though the lost One should be recovered from its dispersion by communication; as though the confusion of the many could resolve itself into rest through conjunction; as though a forgotten truth could never again be wholly attained.

Or, Truth lies in the future. In temporal existence, to be sure, there is an awareness of limits: what is not communicable is as though it were not, since it is not for any consciousness or knowledge. But precisely in communication the drive goes out beyond these limits, not at all to fall back into stupor, but to go onwards into unlimited disclosure so that what is can show itself by entering into communication. But then the drive goes beyond the greatest existential clarity, for there always remains something unsatisfied in it. The high moments of seemingly perfect agreement of communication in the thoroughgoing presence of all modes of the Encompassing, of the knowable, and of Transcendence show themselves even in time either to be false, or to be seeds again for new efforts toward disclosure, toward continuity in time. They are like anticipations of a possible fulfilled communication, which would mean at the same time completed truth and a timeless unity of the soul and the cosmos. The idea of such an unreality as a communication which reaches its goal means the elevation of communication into a transcendent perfection where there is no longer any need to communicate. The question whether, insofar as we have an unlimited will-to-communicate out of Existenz and reason, we do not already live out of this guiding and communicationless Being—such a question is not to be answered. Either the question asks something that is for us perfectly empty or it becomes an unquestionable certitude which dispenses with communication and, falsely expressed, only destroys itself. That is, it would paralyze the working of an unconditioned will-to-communicate by a specious knowledge about perfect communication.

If all communication must be thought of as canceled in Transcendence, as a lack in temporal existence, then all conceivability in general is also canceled. For example, I think upon the old proposition that God is the Truth. Then such a Truth has nothing to correspond with, since it is undivided and without opposition, whereas all other truths are modes of agreement. In fact, such an idea is empty and can only be felt existentially by me historically. Here where I can not penetrate, truth can retain no thinkable sense. The shipwrecking of all thinking about truth can shake one in his depths, but can not provide a tenable thought.

The stillness of the being of truth in Transcendence—not by abandoning the modes of the Encompassing, but in surpassing their worlds—such is the boundary where what the Whole is beyond all division can momentarily flash out. But this illumination is transitory in the world and, although of decisive influence upon men, incommunicable; for when it is communicated it is drawn into the modes of the Encompassing where it is ever lacking. Its experience is absolutely historical, in time out beyond time. One can speak out of this experience, but not of it. The ultimate in thinking as in communication is silence.

X

fourth lecture

THE PRIORITY AND LIMITS OF RATIONAL THOUGHT

The question of the priority of thought

The modes of the Encompassing are: i) as the Encompassing which we are: empirical existence, consciousness as such, and spirit; ii) as Being itself: world and Transcendence. They have their roots in Existenz, their bond in reason. Insofar as we are objects of investigation to ourselves, empirical existents, we are ourselves world; here the Encompassing which we are intersects with the Encompassing which is Being itself insofar as it appears as world.

When we inquire into the priority of one of the modes, it seems that the Encompassing is conceived by us as in levels, and in levels of such a sort that the earlier lose substance without the later, while the later without the earlier are without actuality. To be sure, Transcendence has priority in being; but it is hidden. None of the other modes of the Encompassing can claim an absolute priority in being; each is indispensable in the whole—a whole, moreover, which is no mere sum of levels, but an internally articulated structure of modes of Being—and each mode belongs to the cryptogram of Transcendence.

But there is a hierarchy, surely of Existenz over empirical existence and over spirit, and of spirit over consciousness as such. If we were to express the meaning of this hierarchy in terms such as, "in case of conflict the higher rank should prevail," we would not have touched the real issue. For there are conflicts only on the same level. In order to come into conflict, the meaning of the higher must appear in a form which can enter into that of the lower, where it can touch another form which in itself would be as nothing without power from above. More occurs in the struggle for existence than mere struggle for existence; and in spiritual conflict, more than this alone; the event of existential communication opens a view into Transcendence. The question of the hierarchy of the modes of the Encompassing is an ontological question, and not one merely of the comparative values of modes of Being or of their possible conflict which is never possible anyway except on the level of one of the modes.

To speak of the priority of thought has a totally different meaning. Thought has a formal priority, not a priority in being or value. The priority of thought means that no mode of the Encompassing can be present to us or becomes effective in us unless its content enters into the medium of thought.

While the Encompassing in all its modes is more than mere thought, thought has its formal priority, firstly, because it penetrates everywhere, because nothing can withdraw itself from its contact. Everything else becomes the matter, impulse, meaning and goal, content and fulfillment of thought. Even though the actual existence of all modes of the Encompassing has priority over thought which is dependent upon them, is animated by them, and draws its objects from them, still this priority itself is first brought to light and to its full range as though to its origins by thought. Nothing can withdraw itself from the universality of thought. It is thought which turns everything else into a possibility for us. Its origins are disclosed and its suitable development permitted by thought. There is nothing which can come into appearance without thought.

Secondly, in addition to this power of rendering things present, thought has priority because it is the only medium through which the modes of the Encompassing can become related to one another. There is never a single, true, and finally correct form of the Encompassing in time. Thought is the thorn which forces them to order themselves one to the other; thought is the medium of movement in the Whole.

The universality of thought is not merely a fact of human nature, but a demand made by its freedom upon itself. But this universality can appear as a fatality because, through the formal priority of thought, everything can become evacuated into the mere form of the thinkable, and humanity can be dissolved into the empty play which universally touches upon everything without penetrating into anything, or becoming anybody. The originally positive aspect of opening up possibilities becomes in formalization something negative which destroys everything serious in reality. But now, if one turns against thought, the struggle can only succeed by thought. The destruction of thought always remains itself still thought, but now violent, simplistic, narrow, and self-blinding thought. The fate of thought is the destiny of our humanity; the danger that lies therein is in the unceasing questioning over the path of fulfillment toward a reality which has come to itself and been awakened into development, possibilities first liberated by thought itself.

The formal priority of thought is destroyed in its formalization but is real in the priority of rational thought.

The universality of thought might seem to be identical with the mode of the Encompassing which is consciousness as such. And in fact the form of thought has its origin here. It is not merely identical with it, but is consciousness as such transcending itself. That there is this transcending, that universality is willed radically, arises, not from consciousness as such, but from the totality of the modes of the Encompassing which we are. They all push toward the light through which they first genuinely come into being; all are reason in this sense. Thus, they want to become clear, they want to become whole in relation to all the modes of the Encompassing; they will the universal in some sense, to come under law and order.

But this is only possible because even what is non-rational in this sense is affected by reason. It first becomes being-for-us by being affected by reason. The non-rational acquires being and meaning for us only through its connection with reason. Reason is the indispensable. Thus, I perceive ignorance itself through knowledge, and perfect ignorance only through the maximum of reason. The universality of thought, insofar as it is not formalized but is engaged and filled with content, is reason itself.

Therefore, while the modes of the Encompassing might find their fulfillment in clarity, totality, in the universal, in law and order—reason, although it pushes them on this way, itself is beyond them not only because it can find satisfaction in no clarity, whole, or order, but also because it is open to the essentially unclear, the genuinely fragmentary, and to the non-rational itself.

That which is logically graspable, consistent, univocally present to consciousness as such is rational in the narrowest sense, the understandable. What is a-logical to the understanding, the Other at the limits of understanding, must itself be felt as rational.

We only grasp the a-logical in transcending. We are natures which not only inquire into the things in the world, but also into ourselves and into the Whole. Thus, to be sure, we are real only as empirical existents, as consciousness as such, and as spirit; but therein we are also beyond ourselves and beyond every determinate mode of our empirical existence, beyond every determinate content of thought, and in this "beyond" we first come to ourselves and to Transcendence.

Already in the merely logical explication of the Encompassing which we have tried, we have transcended in thought toward that which can not be objectified, toward that which passes beyond every determinate objectivity. For the clarification of the modes of the Encompassing, we have used words and concepts which had their original meaning for definite things in the world; now however they are used to go beyond the limits and are not to be understood in their original sense, but rather as objectifying aids in bringing the non-objective, the Encompassing to expression.

The question is what this transcending thought means. It should have an influence upon inner life; it aims at making communicable the non-objective, that which does not appear like things in the world. It is only for consciousness as such that the object of thought is directly intelligible simply as the presence of the object or concept, as identical for every understanding, and whose concrete content is given through what can be perceived and through the trivialities of what can be identically and universally felt by everybody. In transcending thought, on the other hand, comprehension is only possible through an encounter in real experience of that Encompassing about which one is talking.

The communicability of thought which passes beyond the understanding of consciousness as such comes to forms which eventually run counter to the understanding. Through reason, I catch sight of something which is only communicable in the form of contradiction and paradox. Here a rational a-logic arises, a true reason which reaches its goal through the shattering of the logic of the understanding.

What is intended through these objectifications, which never mean themselves, can be misunderstood if one tries to grasp it immediately and directly. It is a basic error of the mere understanding to suppose that to enter into thought is to be made thinkable for consciousnss as such. But if transcending expression is taken in direct literalness for consciousness as such, its real meaning will be missed. Here a false logic arises, an untrue reason in the shape of a logic of the understanding.

Indirect expression is to be made logically clear through what is a-logical to the understanding, and here there is a perpetual possibility of misunderstanding in which all that goes beyond the contents of consciousness as such becomes a supposedly known object. What may be senseless for the understanding can be a necessary form of sense; and that which to the understanding seems literal can be a total perversion of the meaning of what is intended.

Thought seems to have its power by restricting itself to the validities of consciousness as such, through its identical, universal spread among all understandings, through the technical mastery of the known; in contrast, transcending thought seems impotent. It is impotent, first of all, in its form of thinking the unthinkable: it always seems to be canceling itself. It is impotent, secondly, in its inadequate objectification of its transcending contents when it thinks it can apply these contents in argument or technique. Thus transcending thought experiences in confusion the ruinous consequences of a perversion which seeks to use what is impotent for consciousness as such. But in spite of all impotence, this thought has a power which can be neither willed nor controlled by technique, a power which can silently bring forth a revelation and transformation in the most interior being of man.

From the immeasurable field of logical clarity in transcending and absolutely universal thought—thought about which alone it can be said that nothing is for us unless it enters into thought—we should now like to show in examples the two directions we have already characterized: i) rational a-logic; ii) false logicizing.

I. A. Rational a-logic; the circle as a necessary form of genuine philosophy.

We shall start with a Kantian idea. Kant conceived all objectivity as a material formed by the categories of the subject which was consciousness as such. We live in a world of appearance produced by us not, to be sure, in its empirical existence, but in its general form. The thing-in-itself was absolutely hidden, a mere limiting concept implied by the phenomenality of empirical existents. Now the categories like unity, plurality, substance, causality, etc., were for Kant to be derived from the original unity of the thinking consciousness, the so-called unity of transcendental apperception which bound whatever we might encounter into the unity of an object. But Kant said, "this unity which precedes a priori all synthesizing concepts is not at all the category of unity." Kant thus requires us in thinking by categories—and, according to him, we can not think otherwise—to grasp something which does not fall under the categories. This he had to do since he wanted to touch the origin of all objectivity which itself could not be objective. Thus, I must think a non-objectivity objectively, that which grounds the categories, including that of unity, under the category of unity. We arrive thus in formal logic either at a circle: unity is explained through unity; or at a contradiction: unity is not unity.

In all genuine philosophies we find such circles and contradictions at the decisive point, whether it is metaphysics, transcendental philosophy, or the clarification of Existenz. And everywhere one sees the critics at work triumphantly exposing these discrepancies and imagining the criticized philosophy thereby destroyed.

But it must be shown that such forms of thought are necessary in philosophy by the nature of things. And, in order to do this, we will first look at the process by which these circles and contradictions arise, according to a purely logical interpretation. To be sure we shall not be interested in those many mistakes which can be corrected verbally without further change, but rather in errors which appear to be logically unavoidable and irresolvable.

There are many striking examples from antiquity. Epimenides the Cretan said, "All Cretans always lie when they speak." Thus, that which Epimenides, a Cretan, said is not true; thus his proposition, "all Cretans lie," is not true, etc. Or there is the story of the sophist Protagoras and his pupil Euathlus who took lessons from him but was to pay only when he had won his first lawsuit. But Euathlus took no cases. When Protagoras brought suit for his money, Euathlus explained: "If I win this suit, I need not pay, for the judgment is against you; and if I lose the suit, I also need not pay since our agreement was that I must pay only on winning my first suit." Or there is the argument of the crocodile: a crocodile stole a child from its mother and told the mother, "I will give it back to you if you will give me the right answer to the following question: Will I give you back your child?" The mother replied, "You will not return my child; and now you must give it back to me in either case. For if my answer was right, then you must return it according to our agreement. And also if it was wrong, for it would be wrong only if you did return my child." But the crocodile answered, "I can not return the child in either case. For if your answer is wrong, then the child is not returned according to our agreement, and if your answer is right, then it is right only if I do return the child."

Without going into the particularities and necessarily

more precise conceptions in these examples, we find as the general principle of the difficulties that in each case there is a so-called self-reflexivity. The lying Cretan says something whose content cancels the saying of it, which is then restored ad infinitum. The object of the trial of Euathlus and the content of the mother's assertion are both condition and conditioned. But we can only think meaningfully and unambiguously if in the content of our thought we have two terms to be related; thus, in the relation of condition, the conditioning and the conditioned must be distinct, and in the relation of object, the thing and its properties must be distinct. The error lies, not in the individual conclusions, but in the premises where only a single term is related to itself. As soon as two are distinguished, all the difficulties fall away, as well as the wit in these oddities invented by the Greeks. These striking examples are so easily grasped that the solution is easy. But we are interested, not so much in these examples, as in the principle to be grasped through them: of a limit to literal conceivability for us.

Now precisely in distinction from cognition of things in the world, in philosophizing something is thought which, if it is to be touched upon, can permit nothing outside of its being thought, since it is the fundamental origin; it may be Being itself, or the condition of all objectivity as in the Kantian philosophy, or it may be Existenz. We always have something which the understanding can not grasp but which is decisive for our certainty of being, which is less before us than present in our thought. The difficulties of formal logic with respect to self-reflexivity must arise. If we make the content of such philosophical ideas one relative term alongside of others, which we must do when we make assertions, then, as so expressed, it is no longer of philosophical content. Therefore such assertions must be made reflexive. Thus, in general, the thinking of that which is inaccessible to the understanding takes on the appearance of a logical impossibility or insolubility, where what is asserted as the supposed cognition of something cancels itself out. Only thus can we reach the point where the essential sense of philosophical thinking is not displaced by a false insight of the mere understanding.

In this double fashion, we can now understand what we often experience in philosophical study. The result of philosophizing is no statable ultimate insight but rather an accomplishment of thought in which our total consciousness, the way in which Being is present to us, is changed.

And all philosophy which wishes to improve itself into an unambiguous communication of knowledge by removing its apparent circles and contradictions falls, so to speak, flat on its face and becomes totally empty.

The critique of philosophy therefore has as its task not the removal of its circles and contradictions, but rather the bringing of them to light in order to see whether they are significant or merely empty circles. For the form of the circle in fact returns in every philosophy, be it ever so confused.

If, for example, a materialist explains the external world as a creation of our physiological organization, more particularly our brain, still the brain, including his own, is a part of the external world which can be observed under local anesthesia, with a trepanation and mirrors. Thus the brain becomes a creation of the brain—formally the same mode of thought which describes God as *causa sui*.

It is an interesting and stimulating investigation to follow the circles and other logical difficulties in philosophy and to notice how absurd stupidities have the same logical form for the understanding as a deep contact with the limits.

But philosophical ideas no longer retain their total expressive power when reduced to these bare circles although they are still preserved in seed. They are dissolved in such a bareness as they are in objective knowledge which they are always on the verge of becoming for the mere understanding. We can speak objectively—and we men can not speak otherwise—about the absolutely non-objective only in forms which cancel themselves out as objective.

B. Examples of the a-logical drawn from the clarification of Existenz.

Let us now trace the a-logical form in the province of Existenz-philosophy. Existenz is something which according to its essence is incapable of being established as an empirical existent and which, therefore, can not be discriminated by any objective investigation. Thus it is as though it were not; it is not verifiable as a stable reality in the world.

If I should say, potential Existenz could truly be in an act which is not only not universal, but runs counter to it—such an act being willed out of historical grounds and entering into rationality by itself, i.e., not from the outside by some commandment of God—then what is thus said would be unverifiable. Objectively, one can not distinguish whether it is a case of a brutal will to live based upon itself in arbitrary stubbornness (which can also occur in a negative will to live, in a desparing negation of life), or whether it is an existential will arising out of the bases of concrete history, related to Transcendence in true freedom, and thus open to all rationality although unclear to itself.

Both of these two possibilities in their mere external appearance for the knowledge of consciousness as such look alike, and are to be distinguished only by Existenz which can see in them two things completely and essentially different.

In the same way, it is impossible to distinguish objectively the ability of Existenz to be alone, which is the origin of true communication, from the self-isolation of an empirical existent which will only enter into commerce with others under definitely settled conditions and not into authentic communication. The truth of my communication is decided by whether I can be alone before Transcendence in infinite loneliness yet not be destroyed, but rather keeping my potentialities ready. Man must be capable of being alone if he is to draw power and potentialities from the origins. On the other hand if I withdraw from the difficulties of the world in order to find escape in an impotent denial which is really a non-willing, then I pass into a self-isolation without Transcendence, I rotate about myself in the empirical existence of my feelings and empty boredom.

In the clarification of Existenz, there are necessary modes of expression which, in their paradox, touch indirectly—the only way possible—upon the truth of Existenz. What we have just discussed can then be expressed briefly:

I become bound to the depths of Being in its individual-universal character, become existentially "historical," only if I enter into and accept the restrictions of my empirical existence.

I am only genuinely in communication if I can be alone before Transcendence in my limits and bases.

There are innumerable corresponding clarifications of Existenz which can be crystallized in the following:

In action, I truly accomplish something out of potential Existenz only if I am consciously prepared to accept its shipwreck.

I am genuinely rational only if my whole reason factually and for my knowing is grounded upon unreason.

I believe only through doubting whether I believe.

II. A. False logicizing: the perversion of existential assertions shown in the examples given.

Such assertions are at the same time sources of misunderstanding and perversion. Their meaning would be destroyed, for example, if I now willed the narrow restrictions of my empirical existence, if I willed solitude, shipwreck, the non-rational as such, or doubt.

Thus historicity is true only if, in its acceptance and thereby in the animation of one's own empirical existence, the greatest range of openness for Transcendence is secured. It is untrue—no longer itself but mere empirical existence—when its notion serves only to affirm the restrictions of empirical existence, a life which is precisely non-historical. In this way it would submerge empirical existence into itself in a fruitless anxiety over itself and its value.

Further, if I should take the assertion, "Existenz is only real in communication," look at it, and treat it as something known, and now proceed to make communication the condition of my Existenz, almost reproaching Being if communication is lacking, then it is precisely that I can not enter into communication for I have destroyed my own unconditional readiness by such an inversion, and misused the idea in such a way as to conceal my inability to be alone by a pseudo-communication which is craved, begged for, and forced.

That the whole of my rationality rests upon the basis of non-reason—such a phrase does not assert that reason can be denied out of some general right drawn from existential philosophy. Nothing which lacks reason or which is contrary to reason can raise up argumentative claims out of itself, for precisely in this process it enters into the medium of rationality. Neither the positivity of mere empirical existence, nor that of the existential basis has a right without reason. Every premise of justification enters into the realm of the rational. The truth of the non-rational is impossible unless reason is pushed to its limit.

Thus, the concepts of existential philosophy can become a medium which confuses Existenz instead of illuminating it. Every direct usage of these concepts as contents of assertions, instead of living under their appeal, is already on this path.

For example, it can be almost the extreme of merciless cruelty to demand freedom of others where it can never be released from its bonds by such direct volition, but only through the ripening prudence of a love which however is unrelentingly demanding. It is as when love is paralyzed and nothing is left but the deadly, abstract demands expressed in rationalistic existential concepts; it is perhaps a priest who is acting, prepared with the means of grace of his church, trying to be of some help even in the extremities. Likewise it is an existentially disastrous refusal if this love, become weak and self-satisfied, deceiving both the other and itself, justifies the other in his empirical existence and shrinks back from the danger of entering into a desperate situation. The misuse of existential concepts by employing them to justify an empirical existence without Existenz also helps this evasive attitude. If the true love is no longer active, a love which first becomes wholly alive in that hard, almost icy, clarity which is open and opening, and distant from all contempt or malice, then a diversion into mere organic bonds in anxiety and feeling is promoted.

Thus the concepts of an existential philosophy can become the means by which the existential is lost more than ever in a delusive pretense. When I apply the concepts abstractly, I speak of something which is only further removed by my speech for I am not really on its path. I speak correctly, and at the same time I am, myself, wholly false. Perhaps abstractly I say something decisive, but I say it in such a fashion that concretely it is not only irrelevant but destroyed. The abstract application no longer speaks in the situation.

The reason is that the truth of existential thought never lies in its content as such, but rather in what happens to me in the thinking of it: either in a passion for possibilities which prepares in advance and recalls, or in real communication where what was said comes forth as existentially true in ever unique ways, unplanned out of the absolute consciousness of love. There is always a misuse when what is intended through philosophic contents is used as though it were something known, to be applied and argued about in order to attain some end, instead of producing by such concepts in oneself and in communication something which is man himself and not something meant by him. Such existential thought is either true, and then it is indissolubly connected with the being of the thinker; or it is a content to be known like any other, and then it is false. The concepts of existential philosophy are such that I can not think them without being in them; scientific contents on the other hand are such that I can know them while I myself live in wholly different categories; what I am is irrelevant to scientific knowledge.

B. General formulation.

In general, the truth of assertions which clarify Existenz is always perverted either when their contents are made into something directly known, or when some end is derived from them for a purposing, planning will. It is then that such assertions pass from a rational a-logic to a false logicizing. For the contents of these assertions always contain the residue of something determinate and literal, empirical existence as it were. Then, as a consequence of this misunderstanding, existential concepts are applied so as to subsume under them other men and myself, their conduct and mine; existential clarification is applied like a psychology. But philosophical expression which informs us about Existenz can not comprehend it and communicate it as though it were an empirically existent thing for consciousness as such without falseness, perversion, and the destruction of Existenz itself.

In general then, for the clarification of Existenz, for metaphysics, and for transcending philosophical world-orientation, for all regions of philosophy, the principle holds that, whenever that which philosophically indicates, appeals to, evokes, allows to be seen, renders present, whenever it is handled as a known content in the mere forms of the understanding, it loses precisely that content which was intended in the philosophy. At the same time it is fraudulent to derive therefrom some fixed doctrine as though it were valid for the understanding.

In speaking there is always something inverted, so that the fundamental ground of Being is touched rather by not naming it in my apprehension of it. But again this is true only if I do not intentionally avoid it—an artificial and merely rhetorical and literary technique—but experience it as the absolutely unwilled.

I can only speak of that out of which I live and am, insofar as I miss saying it conceptually and therefore indirectly reveal it.

C. A glance at the false rationalization of the irrational.

In such attempted logical clarifications we find an ominous phenomenon of the human spirit; it has always been there but has grown in the last century, and may be called the rationalization of the irrational. A supposedly omniscient Enlightenment sought the forms of the understanding even in what was alien thereto in order to produce technically what was desired. In its enthusiasm for irrational values and its attempt to deliberately produce what it wanted, there arose however no increase in the true rationality of the world but rather a further destruction of the non-rational by falsifying genuine rationality.

The essential question about human action is: what can be deliberately planned as an end and what not. Or, what can be desired, and what disappears precisely because it is desired. Or, what can be actually attained by planning and what is made impossible precisely because it becomes the end of a plan.

If for example one should propose as his end to become an independent and distinctive personality, one would become an artificial construct of pure masks lacking in reality down to the core, and thus, precisely no personality at all, but instead an anxiously cultivated appearance. Men become personalities only by being concerned with affairs, only by producing something in the world through deed and activity.

As it is with personality, so with all substantial values. One can will out of them, awaken them indirectly, form one's empirical existence in conformity with their standards, but one can not will them. If myth has passed away, it can not be restored through will which can only create false substitutes. If one thinks a new religion is necessary, one can not make one, and every attempt leads to an impotent sham. If I do not love, I can not force myself, or arrange it, or bring it forth through preparations. If I do not believe, it is hopeless to will to believe; thereby I can only produce falseness and confusion in me and my world.

In general, the result of these inversions can only be the helplessness of the understanding itself, an understanding which has isolated itself and thinks it can know and deliberately produce everything.

D. Summary: Priority of thought confirmed.

What we have been explaining through examples should show in what sense one must speak of the priority of thought.

The nature of thought and knowledge is commonly taken in too narrow a sense, that of an understanding which exhausts itself in mechanical thinking, distinguishing, defining, and ordering. To experience such narrow, formalized, and partial thought is to furnish from thinking the basis for confusion out of which the impulse arises to reject thought as destructive of life.

But even if I take thought in the wider sense of any objective or objectified dialectical thought, intellectually I experience this: what I know, insofar as it is known, actually becomes relativized for me since it changes into a possibility, into something questionable. Thus it seems that I can not both unconditionally be and, at the same time, know it. Hence the question arises whether we can remain true to our fundamental basis if we extend our knowledge out endlessly.

In fact we remain true to our fundamental basis and bound to Being only if we dare the utmost in knowability, for only then are the bases unfolded and Being revealed. But also, we remain true to these bases only if we do not abandon ourselves to the mere forms of speech and to the forms of the superficially thinkable, when we do not permit ourselves to think without matter or content. This again demands a continuous restriction and control by thinking itself: we only remain true, then, when we are really conscious of the modes of knowing and their limits. There is no truth without some kind of communicability, and what is communicable always belongs on many levels to the various modes of the Encompassing in their interrelations, and always has its meaning within its sphere, not outside of it.

Therefore, how I understand my knowing is a basic question of philosophizing from its inception on. It is the self-consciousness of reason.

The detachment from the finite known by understanding this knowing first brings the determinate known really near and, at the same time, frees Existenz from the merely known in which Existenz is always in danger of losing itself as though in Being. The thoroughgoing penetration of this knowing about knowing alone can open up our consciousness of Being to the ever-present Transcendence in a way which is not deceptive.

E. Two misunderstandings of the expression of this priority; empty logic and absolute knowledge.

But the knowledge of knowledge from Aristotle up to the transcendental thought of Kant runs into two typical errors. First of all it runs into the vacuity of a logic which is empty because it has no relation to Being. Therewith it becomes terrified when it finds itself entering into the endlessness of a new determinate knowledge, an infinity of syllogistic forms, relations among signs, of arbitrary and, not only formal, but empty, operations. Then it is no longer a knowing which penetrates through all particular knowledge with a consciousness of Being itself, but a philosophically indifferent knowledge of possible forms of expression, intellectualities, verbalisms, mathematically graspable formalisms. The authentic knowing of knowing, although it must also go along these paths in order to master these materials, is not a determinate knowledge itself, but rather a knowledge of the modalities of determinate knowledge. Such a penetrating knowledge no longer exists when it is abstracted from determinate knowledge, but is then hollowed out and itself becomes simply a new kind of determinate knowledge.

Secondly, this abstraction occurs through an opposite kind of misunderstanding, in the "absolute knowledge" of idealism. The error of idealism consists in changing a consciousness of Being, which is illuminated by penetrating the whole of knowledge in all modes of the Encompassing, into an isolated generation of what is in fact a determinate knowledge of everything. Such a knowledge wanted to be constructed independently and abstractly like some mathematics, as though it could create its own contents by itself. As such it was to have ended up in the completion of a system in which everything real, the Godhead itself, was to have become known.

Both misunderstandings are only an indication of a Substance whose misunderstanding first makes them possible. Here is a source out of which all knowledge can be enlivened into a consciousness of Being. Or, here is a spring from which knowledge can, in the knower, acquire the impulse to become more than the mere knowledge of something by becoming knowledge of the modes of knowledge.

What this is can only be enacted in thinking; it can not in turn come to be known again as an individual. Thought recalls it and pushes toward it.

Instead of there being a demand for universal and unlimited thinking which as such leads into emptiness and infinity, there is a demand to think out of reality, out of Being itself, and by thought to advance on back into Being. It is not sufficient to say: be rational! but rather: be rational out of Existenz, or better, out of all the modes of the Encompassing.

Again however this is not to be attained by deliberate willing. Rather one encounters in that inner act which is genuine philosophizing something like this: when in philosophizing the point is reached where everything stops, where the self sees itself before nothingness or the divinity, then it is important for the movement of thought as far as it can not to sink through the vacuum into the absolutely groundless, but rather to hold the thinker open for the encounter with Being which only becomes perceptible to each when he comes upon himself, does not leave himself out, and, so to speak, is given to himself.

Here at the most extreme limits, however, the understanding, as the will toward the intuition of something determinate, toward graspability, toward the deliberate willing of an end, has its own impulse. At this point where everything has become empty, nothingness, it substitutes a particular real thing from the world of finite knowledge for a transcendent, fulfilled historicity. That is, instead of becoming aware of the growth of the authentic being of Transcendence in a philosophical movement of Existenz, rather it psychologizes, sociologizes, naturalizes.

To protect itself against the absolutization of limited, empirical things in the world, the known and investigable, to hold itself free for Transcendence, and to preserve itself from the empty understanding and the endless formalization of speech which no longer comprehends, thought in its priority must actually be achieved in the clarity of unlimited, and yet always determinate, knowledge of knowledge; it must always reason in order to perceive that which is more than reason.

fifth lecture

POSSIBILITIES FOR CONTEMPORARY PHILOSOPHIZING

Our situation through Kierkegaard and Nietzsche: the problem: not to philosophize as an exception but in the light of the exception

In the first lecture we saw how Kierkegaard and Nietzsche created the actual situation for philosophizing in this epoch. Because of them the powers and necessities of thought are in a new situation which has arisen in a manner historically unique and incapable of being understood by analogy with any other historical fact. To be sure, these philosophers have been indignantly discarded from time to time. But since they have not really been penetrated nor seen in their true reality and thought, they keep returning, greater and more impressive than before. Their ambiguous influence has lasted through half a century, as stimulating as it is radically destructive.

Philosophically we had to protect ourselves against their becoming misunderstood, against the nihilistic, sophistically perverting manner of using their ideas and words, a manner which misleads into endless reflection or mere suggestive surprises, in order to experience more decisively the indispensable demand which they left behind.

We have seen in the past decades an impotent and fruitless restriction of truth to the so-called rational truth which is only speciously rational, and then we have seen an equally fruitless rejection of reason into which the reliance upon an insufficiently understood reason easily turns. But the philosophy which today is called Existenz-philosophy[1] in this light is not on the side of the chaotic and irrational movements, but rather should be seen as a counterblow to them; and the chaotic and ruinous can just as easily appear in the deceptive garments of rationality as in a frank irrationalism. In Existenz-philosophy, out of the decisiveness of our fundamental bases, the clarity of a life related to Transcendence should again become communicable in thought, as a philosophizing with which we actually live.

To ask again in the contemporary philosophic situation, what is philosophy? what will become of philosophy? means that we think we are in fact at an end. Hegel was the end of Western philosophy, of objective, confident, absolute rationality, and recent philosophizing in the manner of Hegel is a contemporary knowledge about the totality of a past reality. Kierkegaard and Nietzsche exhausted the possibilities of questioning, the questioning by exceptions in endless reflection standing outside communication, alone with God or nothingness. The study in their principles of both sorts of termination has become the condition, not only of acquiring the intellectual means for philosophizing, but also essentially of avoiding superficial and easy affirmations of nothingness, and of coming inwardly in one's own experience to the point where one really knows that here he can go no further. In fact we are not standing before nothingness, but rather, as always where men are living, before our fundamental bases. From such experience the new philosophizing grows of whose potentialities we shall now sketch a picture.[2]

Philosophy after Kierkegaard and Nietzsche can no longer bring its thought into a single, complete system to be brought out as a presentation derived from its principles. It is a question of letting those principles themselves become effective. The problem for us is to philosophize without being exceptions, but with our eyes on the exception.

The truth in the exception for us is that it poses a perpetual question without which we would sink back into the more or less crude platitudes of a self-satisfaction which is no longer thinking radically. Through a knowledge of exceptions, our souls instead of incapsulating themselves in narrowness can remain open to the possible truth and reality which can speak even in despair, suicide, in the passion toward Night, in every form of negative resolution. To see rationally what is counter-rational shows us not only the possibility of a positive side in the negative, but also the ground on which we ourselves stand. An indispensable approach to the truth would be lost without the exceptions. Their earnestness and absoluteness overpower us as standards although we do not follow them in their content. That we owe something new to Kierkegaard and Nietzsche—the possibility of laying the deepest foundations—and yet that we do not follow them in their essential decisions, makes up the difficulty of our philosophical situation.

The philosophizing which owes its impulse to them will, in opposition to their lack of communication, be a communicative philosophizing (or it would be labor lost, since the exception can not be repeated). Against the negative, unlimited radicality of the exception, it will be bound in the communicability of all modes of the Encompassing. Against their risks of worldlessness, it will not only be a weakening, but issue forth from a will to connection in communication as an historical task.

This attitude is shown in some preliminary, necessary features of contemporary philosophizing:

1. Since it is not to be a philosophy of the exception, but of the universal, it will only regard itself as true if it can be translated into reality by many, that is, if the possibility

of reason in its widest range is methodically brought to self-consciousness.

2. Only in the light of the exception which did the seemingly impossible can we find our way back without deception to a universality in the history of philosophy, which thereby once again becomes transformed.

3. In view of the exception whose thinking in fact is not only philosophizing, but almost turns into non-philosophy (whether into a faith in revelation or into atheism), philosophy must become aware of moving between these two possibilities, which both concern it and call it into question.

4. Therewith must philosophy again ascertain the ground of its own philosophic faith.

It is as though we again sought on these paths of philosophizing the quietude of Kant and Spinoza, of Nicolas of Cusa and Parmenides, turning away from the ultimate unrest of Kierkegaard and Nietzsche. But still these latter philosophers remain as lighthouses still burning, perpetual indicators of directions without which we would relapse into the deception of supposing there were a teachable philosophic doctrine or contents, which as such are without power.

1. REASON AND PHILOSOPHICAL LOGIC.

The great philosophical concern was always and has again become reason. After the questioning of Kierkegaard and Nietzsche, reason is no longer self-evident to us. The deepest fathoming of reason in the philosophy of German idealism is no longer persuasive, although it remains an unexhausted source of a rationality without which we would not have reached the level of genuine philosophical thought.[3]

If, looking back at the actual philosophizing of the centuries, we ask whether philosophy can ground itself upon reason, the answer must be no, since, in all the modes of the Encompassing, through reason it grounds itself upon some other, finally essentially upon Transcendence; and also yes, since the way in which it does ground itself leads only above reason. Philosophy does not live by reason alone, yet it can take no step without it.

Reason is not quite the substance out of which philosophy arises. For philosophy must ground itself in potential Existtenz, which, for its part, can only unfold in rationality. I am that which is capable of reason but which is not made up of pure reason. If reason is not substantial, it is also true that nothing else is substantial without reason as its condition.

I can speak of Reason, personify it, and pay my respects to it as the condition of all truth for me. But it is never a permanent thing; rather it constitutes a continuous task in time. It is not an end in itself, but rather a medium. It is that through which everything else preserves its nature, is clarified, corroborated, and recognized. It is as though without reason everything were asleep like a seed.

I can produce nothing by reason alone. I must always encounter in it that other through which it itself is. This can be shown in every action of reason. Nothing real can merely be excogitated; and therefore Transcendence, for example, can not be proven. But the pure thinking of reason which is not valid as the determinate knowledge of anything (which determinate knowledge always depends upon something else through its intuition or its mere givenness) —such reason is itself an act of Existenz in a particular form. Existenz in a self-positing cognition of its own Transcendence is a thinking which as such is an experience of its own being: that which is unavoidably connected with the consciousness of my Existenz is not thereby proven for the understanding as such, but exists for this Existenz which is clarifying itself validly in reason. Reason works a proof for the existence of God out of the factual presupposition of divinity, a proof which lacks any logically abstractable evidence indeed, but which nevertheless is fulfilling and inspiring for Existenz.

It is the nature of reason to be uncreative in itself, and precisely for this cause it can be universal, and through its universality it can bring the creative everywhere into act. There is nothing which can withdraw itself from contact with reason, and nothing which does not authentically emerge for the first time through either the positive or negative conditions of reason.

The self-consciousness of this universal rationality is formally developed as philosophical logic.

We have attempted in the preceding lectures to sketch three ideas in this field in order to clarify what looks like a conflict between reason and Existenz in falsifying simplifications: the broadening idea of the Encompassing; the binding idea of truth as communicative; and the idea of the pre-eminence of thought which shows the universal presence of reason, a reason which includes the counter-rational and makes even falsehood possible. There is always a polarity of reason and Existenz, a polarity which is only an abbreviated formula for a complex of interrelated modes of the Encompassing as that which we are and in which being is for us.

If we have followed along these paths in philosophical logic, then, in accordance with logical consciousness, it is no longer possible to possess the truth in some point of view, or in the form of mutually antithetical and exclusive or resolved possibilities. Empirical existence is, so to speak, broken up so that there we have to struggle for truth in the modes of the Encompassing, a truth which is always fighting against itself, and on paths whose origin and final goal are not known. Thus there can be no doctrine which is the solution, which one can now accept as the truth, since such a thing would directly destroy the problem of men living in time.

It is necessary to break through every form which tends

to become a final validity, to master all thinkable points of view in their relativity; and it is necessary to be present consciously in all modes of the Encompassing, to complete all modes of communicability. In this fashion alone is that space to be secured in which the fundamental basis of Existenz can truly be a support.

The total problem of philosophical logic which has been represented in the three lectures above as examples can now be made clearer. This logic is no longer to be limited to the traditional formal logic or to methodology of investigation and proof in the sciences; these partial fields remain intact in their detail, though not in their total meaning. What Kant's transcendental logic, taken in its widest sense, initiated is a new, and ever since indispensable, basis. What Hegel developed in his metaphysical logic as a categoriology, even if inacceptable in principle and development, is nevertheless a solution to a problem related to our contemporary one: the problem of a logic of human thinking in every form of the Encompassing.

The traditional school logic has not discriminately surveyed the manifold of logical possibilities with an openness to all modes of the Encompassing. It was throughout bound to the rationally objective or its simple opposite. It unified itself by a narrow absolutization. Philosophical logic, on the other hand, must let the knowledge of the modes of the Encompassing in their levels and spheres effectively emerge against any leveling of thought (in kinship with the ancient and ever-recurring doctrine of levels of Being). But it must also oppose the attempt to become organized itself as though such a thing could ever be completed. It is indeed the only analogue still possible to the summa, for it has a consciousness of the whole even if only in the form of communicability; but it itself can never become a totality.

Philosophical logic owes this new possibility to Kierkegaard and Nietzsche. What these two did and partly became aware of (Kierkegaard more than Nietzsche), and what they clarified in systematic rationality is still the unresolved problem.

This new logic took its impulse from Existenz which sought its own clarity, but which remained unsatisfied by every attempted rational solution. In contrast to Existenz-philosophy, which goes into the possibilities of the self, it is a path to the self-awareness of reason in the universality of thought. That is, it is a rational concern to penetrate the forms and methods which are always unconsciously generated in all modes of ontological investigation, in the sciences, in philosophical world-orientation, in Existenz-philosophy, and in metaphysics.[4]

The meaning of this logic is negative insofar as it generates no new contents, but positive insofar as it establishes space for every possible content. It holds up clear delimitations against the danger of the loss of some sense of truth or some possible content. In a bewildering confusion of assertions, it brings about clarity of consciousness. And thereby, it prevents the transformation of men into mere empirical existents where unclear impulses, influences, transpositions, and concealments extinguish the possibility of any substantial selfhood—empirical existents for which, in the end, psychoanalysis would be the correct theory. By its openness to the exception it safeguards every kind of knowable in the sense of its particular contents against mere rhetoric and false absolutization. Thus philosophical logic can be an objectively powerless, unforced, and quiet operation through which truth in every one of its senses is enabled to grow out of its origins. Consciousness of the modes of knowing encourages every mode to work itself out resolutely. Thus philosophical logic is the form of honesty grown conscious.

Philosophical logic further is of assistance to communication. Rational logic alone is still an instrument which carries with it the most extreme danger of breaking off communication. If truth is bound to communicability, then, first of all, a common clarity, continuously renewed in the logical and in general in every mode of the Encompassing, is the presupposition of methodical mutual communication. But secondly, while in general speech all modes of meaning speak through one another, it is precisely where the contents no longer bind us together as obvious that the problem of logic becomes of increased importance. Filling the conditions of logical insight as such is not yet sufficient for existential communication; the conditions can be fulfilled, and yet the contents can divide us. Still, through logical clarity we can always meaningfully speak with one another; through it radically alien natures can still try to communicate fruitfully and with stimulation across the abyss.

For there lies in rationality, when it is grasped in its radicality, multidimensionality, and in its connection with Existenz, a trust in itself, as though it must always still be possible. How far it actually succeeds however is a matter of experience. It becomes irrational when it tries to anticipate. Rather its own reason forbids it from presupposing itself unquestioningly. But even if it finally found no echo in all the world, it still could not despair in itself. For it alone can see both itself and its alternatives, can clarify the ultimate shipwreck and the absolutely irrational in their rationality, and thereby first let them emerge into being.[5]

2. THE APPROPRIATION OF THE PHILOSOPHICAL TRADITION.

The rational will for the universal places under question the knowledge about a supposedly absolute end which came in, perhaps, with Hegel, Kierkegaard, and Nietzsche. Such a will turns back to its own fundamental origins and therewith to its own history. Against the nihilism of total rejection and ignorant recommencements, its origin and history become problematic to it in new ways. If Kierkegaard's and Nietzsche's ideas and Existenzen have revolutionized us, we come to insights whose contents we can recognize retrospectively in the philosophizing of the past.

We want to understand authentically once again what had already been done but which remained without final methodical awareness. We believe we can trace with greater awareness the sources of eternal philosophizing, the *philosophia perennis*, and separate more clearly genuine philosophizing from rational vacuities. A new history of philosophy which speaks existentially is arising for us which can preserve the ancient philosophy more truly because more inwardly than before.

The last few centuries were characterized by the frequency with which philosophers thought they were beginning totally *de novo*, so that there was always a new philosopher arising to claim that with him scientific philosophy began for the first time. We think and see the matter otherwise. The recurrent originality of philosophizing is nothing but an appropriation of the truth which is already there, so to speak, although it is always in a communicative process as an historical accomplishment. Indeed, the preservation of the tradition of our fathers is authentic only through a comprehension of the contemporary situation, not through an identical repetition of what they said, nor through an adherence to their words which ignores the contemporary—as though what were past could directly be real and true today. But, even with total changes of the human situation, something deeply hidden and inward remains the same ever since man began to philosophize. Demonstrations of what is new and not to be found in the past concern, for the most part, only forms of expression, historically determined impulses, methods of approach, historical contents—comings and goings which are the indispensable contingent form and repository of the Unconditioned, but also the form of what is immediately worthy of love. As God can not be a developing nature but yet must come to himself, so, from the beginning, philosophizing is a union with the One through the searching thought of existing men, an anchor which is thrown down and which each throws as himself. Even the greatest men do not throw it for others.

3. PHILOSOPHY BETWEEN REVEALED FAITH AND ATHEISM.

Kierkegaard and Nietzsche are distinguished from the other great philosophers in that both consciously subverted philosophy itself: one in favor of faith in absurd paradox and martyrdom as the only true life, the other in order to arrive at atheism. Together they make clear what can befall philosophy because it is not the only possibility open to men. The philosophizing Existenz is found in its pure origins only insofar as it sees itself confronting another reality which is not true for itself, but only for that other: before revealed religion[6] and before atheism. This alternative to philosophy on both its sides—the obedient, churchly belief of cults, and atheism—is a reality of world-dominating importance. Both attest to their truth through acts of sacrifice and consuming passions even though, like philosophy itself, among the masses they dissolve into comfortable custom, untroubled indifference, and formalistic talk.

That the philosopher has lost his enclosed, self-sufficient truth means, at the same time, an openness for what he is not. In history only among philosophizing men do we find that dissatisfaction, that readiness to hear, that courage of thought which shrinks back before nothing, through which also they are always transcending what they have found so as to approach even closer to the truth and avoid masking it with anticipations and finalities. Their attitude can look like insecurity since they do not dogmatically claim possession of the truth; but this unsureness is in fact the sign of their power in unrelenting search, which alone can make possible that true, unrestricted communication which would bind man together with man beyond all finite purposes, natural sympathies, ideas, or insights.

Thus philosophical truth, as long as it does not go astray, can not be understood as a single and unique truth. It sees its own alternative outside itself, to which it is enduringly related, without either absolutely denying it as falsehood or appropriating it as its own truth.

The idealism in man finds the high standard where he seeks it. As long as we remain serious, we encounter the seriousness of others as important to us. The unconditionally atheistic is closer to the truly faithful than is thoughtless mediocrity. But the philosopher worries unceasingly about these others; he is touched by both churchly religion and by atheism. He searches them out in their highest forms.

It was not always so in the consciousness of philosophy. Medieval philosophy thought of itself as a *praeambula fidei;* atheism was absolutely false, an enemy to be destroyed. Descartes was a true servant of the church under whose conditions alone he wished to philosophize. Spinoza was without enmity to these alternatives, but also without recognition of their possible truth; believing himself in possession of the truth, he was as though blessedly at rest, moving out into the contemplation of God. Hegel translated everything into pure spirit, knew spirit in his own sense down to the bottom, worked out his Logic as a form of divine worship, and thought he was a believing Christian.

Today the question is posed more decisively, with avoidance no longer possible. Philosophizing sees in a more honest way that it is incapable of reaching the meaning of faith in revelation and, against it, asserts its own way of seeking God out of its own resources. It sees itself as imperiled from within by a doubt whose real success would be atheism but which philosophy rejects out of its own grounds.

To this correspond attitudes toward philosophy by these others. Orthodox religion regards philosophy as atheistic, while atheism regards it as a dishonest and impotent impovishment of religion out of whose secularization philosophy rose as a moribund descendent.

Philosophizing however remains true only so long as it stays within its own independent and irreplaceable sources.

Philosophy is never a sociological power like churchly belief and atheism. Powerless, the spirit of philosophy emerges out of its ever-present source in the soul only to awaken the soul and let it participate in a truth which has no "purpose" and which neither serves nor opposes any other truth. Only in its own inwardness does it lead to an experience of the presence of the truth through the path of thinking out of the whole nature of man. It is only comparable to the prayer of religion; but at the same time it is less than prayer since it does not have the definite answer of a personal divinity, and also more than prayer since it is the unrestricted perception of all possibilities of the Encompassing and of their always historically absolute fulfillment in one's own Existenz. Only such is the achievement which is proper to philosophy.

Philosophical thinking however can seek its achievement totally otherwise in priestly religion itself, and then it sinks back into a *praeambula fidei*, imperceptibly preserving its own grounds for a long time in spite of that alien fulfillment which, in itself, would retroactively tend to dry out philosophy into a mere conceptual schematism.

Or, philosophical thinking can seek its realization in atheism which presents itself as the conclusion of a philosophizing which opposes revealed religion; and then, retroactively, philosophy as such tends to be annulled in favor of its finite knowledge of the world. Atheism however applies philosophy, now robbed of its essence, as a disintegrating force against everything permanent or authoritative, so long as this is not the authority affirmed by atheism itself of dominance in empirical existence.

Philosophizing which remains faithful to its origins can not really understand either revealed religion or atheism. Both, insofar as they are modes of thought, appear to develop their ideas in conceptual terms which seem to be analogous to those of philosophy and even for the most part borrowed from it. But in their inner activity, both must work in a way essentially different from this apparent one. The philosopher is perplexed by what is not understood as though by something that decisively concerns him. He does not understand it, since in order to understand one must be it. The man who philosophizes can not know whether one day he will not betray his path and sink to his knees praying, or whether he will not surrender himself to the world in the atheism of: nothing is true, everything is permitted. And this, although he must look upon both alternatives as though they represented the suicide of his nature as eternally bound to Transcendence. In its incomprehension or in its concern over mere accidentals, revealed religion from the philosopher's standpoint has made a *salto mortale* into an inaccessible region from which philosophy itself must appear as something inessential. On the other hand, atheism appears to him as productive of adventurous claims about the course of the world, thoughtless superstitions, uncomprehended substitutions for religion, so that in its fanaticism it seems closer to the intolerantly battling religions of the churches than to philosophy.

Philosophy remains continually confronting these two other modes of belief into which it can change only by giving up its own resources but which it can ignore as indifferent or false only by losing its own life. Its life must ever remain questionable in order to become authentically certain of itself.

The philosopher himself achieves his fulfillment, not by anything abstractly universal in his thought, nor by a restriction to thought as such, but rather in his historicity.

In this historicity he has a positive relation to his own religious origins as well as to the universally penetrating fluid of atheism. Looking at the fact of atheism, he sees a decisive battle over the nature of man which can not help but change into something very different when God becomes alien and dead. Philosophically, however, this battle is not an external one against an appearance in the world but an inner conflict which brings forth those ideas which speak from soul to soul in their union with divinity.

4. PHILOSOPHIC FAITH.

In face of both religion and atheism, philosophy lives out of its own faith. As long as man philosophizes, he knows he stands not in relation to the holy chain of "witnesses to the Truth" (in which the believing Christ dared feel himself to be), nor to that of atheism which has always been effective in the world and spoken out; but rather he is related to the chain of private men who openly search in freedom. The brilliant members of this chain are the few great philosophers who desired no disciples, indeed, disdained them, who were as much aware of their human finitude as of the infinity in which they lived, and who offered the torch to those who reached for it of themselves and, in the end, carried it forth perhaps only as a glimmering spark until the next should kindle it to brighter flame.

This belief which is in reason is more than reason. It is not the same if I base myself absolutely in the self-certitude of reason as a cognizing act, and if I have confidence in this medium as a potentiality of my own Existenz. The kind of philosophizing which always seeks to ground itself in mere reason must also always end in vacuity. In philosophy it is how that which is not reason and through which reason first gains its whole scope is present, which is decisive over the substance of philosophy in its historicity.

What the distinctively philosophic faith is, then, is not to be expressed literally and objectively, but only in an ultimately indirect communication of the total philosophical work. Only the ways in which it appears can be clarified directly by the following considerations. Philosophic faith is the fundamental source of that work by which man makes himself in an inner act as an individual before his Transcendence, stimulated by tradition, but without any rationally definable bond to any particular form. For all philosophizing is unique and unrepeatable, although it is all rooted in one source making every philosophy akin to every other in its form.

If philosophy is the continuous self-education of man as an individual, this individual is not to be understood as a singularity in the objective manifold of endless, distinct empirical existents, but rather as the process of overcoming empirical isolation which in itself leads to nothing but capriciousness and obstinacy. The apparent closeness among individual empirical existents is something destructive to the philosophical Existenz, although if it is melted down into the Encompassing of the one Being, it can become its historical body.

The individual, also, is not himself through differentiation from all others, through greater gifts, creativity, beauty, or will; but the individual is that which every man can be himself and which no one already is by nature. But it is also not to be found in likeness to everyone else; for likeness arises out of comparison. The individual when he is himself, like every other selfhood, is outside comparison, and therefore, as such, is characterized through the fact that he does not compare himself with anything except with Ideas, as standards which are above him, but are not empirical existents. The individual compares himself only in those aspects where he is not properly himself. The individual before his Transcendence, in which position alone man is man, struggles against the evaporation of his own fundamental ground into something universal, but also against his own loss of himself through defiant self-assertion and the anxieties of his empirical singularity.

If philosophic faith has the inner act for its existential axis, then the ideas of a philosophical clarification can help to consummate such faith.

This philosophizing will have much more force to the degree that it can express its truth purely and formally. Through this it acquires an awakening power, since it remains open for achievement by new men in their historicity, but not a bestowing power which rather would only be deception. As in the philosophizing of Kant and back through all the great philosophers, the pure form of thought is what is authentically transforming in him who can think and achieve it.

If a believing and fulfilling philosophy first comes to be through a real Existenz, so also is genuine contemplation an act of Existenz. Philosophical contemplation is the life of Existenz as it ponders over Being, as it reads the cryptograms of empirical existence and all modes of Being which I encounter and which I am. It sinks out of time, so to speak, and sees time itself as a cipher in appearance.

The philosophical ideas, whose realization is the reality of this process and which become empty and mere expressions if separated therefrom, are, so to speak, the music of speculation. In them it is as though there had been an inversion of the exploration of existential possibilities into a contact with the real, as though films had fallen from our eyes not about things in the world as such, but about the Being itself in them and in all possibilities—an experience which is not the cognition of anything in particular but which brings an experience of Being through the very act of thinking. It is like a working of thought which transforms the man but brings forth no object. It passes through the ages like a secret which however is always open to whoever would participate in it, a secret which in every generation can lead again to what has been reported from Parmenides to Anselm: a non-conceptual satisfaction in ideas which to those who do not understand are mere formal abstractions, empty follies.

Objections against this philosophizing

The picture of contemporary philosophizing, as it reveals itself under the determining influence of Kierkegaard and Nietzsche, has been sketched in some of its basic features. Against this philosophizing some typical objections arise:

First of all, one can indicate other origins and subsume it under an historical type. Since thus it would have occurred already and is nothing new, it becomes something old, already refuted or settled in fact, something which has returned in disguise like a worn-out ghost. In this fashion, contemporary philosophy has been called nothing but the old idealism, removed from reality, weak, and deceptive.

To which one may reply that wholesale judgments, if they do not go into the details of the actual thinking, can only subsume schematically. The earnestness of thought which is engaged in contemporary philosophizing is not expressed in such schematisms, but rather the intellect of him who is thinking about it externally. All genuine philosophy becomes idealism from such a point of view. The objector must say what he himself wants and believes: and it will be either religious belief in revelation, or real atheism, or an unphilosophical, positivistic, supposedly realistic, and thoroughly trivial, immanence.

Or, one may object that this philosophy is an attempt to fill up the void to which philosophy as such leads with borrowings from religion. It is a secularization of protestant theology, as has often happened, or even a disguised theology.

But such an objection supposes that the absolutely human must be the distinctively Christian, that the historical must be what is distinctively historical in Christian revelation. It first makes the deceptive presupposition that the human is null and void unless the determinate contents of revelation and grace are effective therein. And then Christianity is falsely brought nearer to us and made easier by supposedly theological thought through a clarification of the human, which is essentially a philosophic, and not yet Christian, faith. Perhaps in such a connection, philosophy is the better theology since it is more honest even if it is negative. It shows how far theology lives from philosophical ideas, which, as its own possession, philosophy will not abandon.

Secondly, some logical objections are raised. The new philosophizing does not want to be science, yet wants to make universally valid assertions. It therefore contradicts itself. And with this is connected its thoroughgoing and vexatious antinomical structure; it takes back what it says—gives and denies.

To which one may reply that this is a question of becoming aware of the logic of philosophizing. In such a logic, certain forms and levels of meaning in communication are differentiated; there is a grasp of the contradiction which is necessary in its place, and of a field distinctive of philosophy which has the significance of something universally established (in philosophical world-orientation, and in philosophical logic).

Further, the objections run to the effect that this philosophizing is incomprehensible, since it wants to grasp the non-objective, which is nonsense. It therefore expresses itself contradictorily in objective terms about that which can never become objective; but where there is nothing objective, there is nothing at all. So this philosophizing is an idle attempt to jump over its own shadow, or following Münchhausen, to lift itself by its own bootstraps. It is nothing but an intellectual acrobatics, alien to life.

Such an objection, to be sure, describes correctly in part, although crudely, a form of communication, but at the same time misses its meaning. Through lack of understanding, the evaluation has not touched upon what is here accomplished. For it is a matter of a mode of transcending, which is indeed meaningless and simply crazy for the finite understanding which would be nothing but finite. But because the finite understanding can not transcend finitude, we can not conclude that such transcending is nothing for the reason in Existenz.

Further, they present us with two alternatives: there is either factual, rationally conceivable, impersonal knowledge of the whole (systematic philosophy) with its meaningful claim to validity for every understanding, or else there is some sort of poetic, artistic work. But this philosophizing is neither of these, and thus either it is nothing at all, or else it is a turbid and incompetent mixture of poetry and rationality.

But the presupposition of this objection—either art or science—is questionable, for it stems from a division of spheres of culture and mind which in no way can claim an exclusive validity. It comes to this: the mode of thought in a philosophy must be methodically grasped in its distinctiveness, seen in its own origins, not as a false intermediary from some other point of view.

Thirdly, certain substantial objections are raised. In this philosophizing all objective applicability and order, and therefore all binding force is canceled. It is unscientific, and therefore subjectivistic, and proceeds from nothing but arbitrary caprice.

Against which it must be explained rather that philosophy passionately seeks an abiding order which would be undeceptively permanent. It recognizes the modes of order and appropriates them, but holds its consciousness open for the limits of every order and therefore open for the ulitmate point of rest which would alone be true and which is not to be anticipated. It is scientific in the sense of a disciplining form of rational communication; but not in the sense of substituting a universally valid and relative scientific validity for an unconditioned historical truth. Precisely this philosophizing alone can preserve the mode of thinking of genuine science, grasp it, and animate it, and therewith extinguish what is unscientific in mere intellectual games, absolutized science and deceptive non-philosophy. It can effect a real conquest over empty intellectualism through an understanding grounded in Existenz. Philosophy demands of its hearers that they encounter it with themselves, selves that it can not give—that, only God can do—but which it can awaken. For it, human thinking, which is all that it is, is only an occasion for the other and not already his fulfillment.

Further, there is the complaint that this philosophy is individualistic.

But this is a radical error. Alternative categories, as mutually exclusive, including those of the individualistic and universalistic, are inapplicable to the level of philosophy, for in this form both lead to error. Philosophy in its formulations can be misused individualistically just as well as universalistically.

Finally, the general objection of subjectivism is expressed in the following form: this philosophy recognizes even the symbols of Transcendence only as subjectively created structures and, therefore, actually misses the being of divinity, just as it misses all objectivity.

In no case does this happen in genuine philosophy. Philosophy in principle recognizes all phenomena as relevant to it only insofar as they can serve as symbols of the prior actuality of Transcendence. In its search, it grasps symbols as possible *vestigia dei*, not God himself in his secrecy. The ciphers mean something for it insofar as they point to what is hidden as the final authentic Being which they can not unveil.

Against objections, philosophy can defend itself logically only in the rare cases where the content of what is said is capable of a cogent, universally valid establishment without other substance being brought in. Otherwise, philosophy can only proceed positively; it speaks and manifests itself in its unfolding. True philosophy is in principle unpolemical. It believes in that out of which it came and in that toward which it moves; it waits for the source in every man. It knows no security and relies only on the quiet manifestation of that truth which is expressed in it.

NOTES

NOTES

FIRST LECTURE

[Those notes giving page references for the citations from Kierkegaard and Nietzsche in their German editions have been omitted in this translation.]

a) For the understanding of both Kierkegaard and Nietzsche it is of importance to study them together and to interpret them mutually. What is common to both is the essential thing: the return to the Existenz of men in this contemporary Western situation.

b) For Kierkegaard, who was thirty years Nietzsche's senior, no influence was possible since he was dead by 1855; for Nietzsche there was no influence since he had not seen a line of the German translation of Kierkegaard, which had already been made by that time. It is interesting to see how Nietzsche, whose attention had been called to Kierkegaard in 1888 by Brandes, planned on his next trip to Germany "to work on the psychological problem of Kierkegaard." Nothing more ever came of this opportunity for Nietzsche to come to terms with his unique relative.

SECOND LECTURE

1) On schemata of the ego, cf. "Existenzerhellung," pp. 27 ff., in my *Philosophie* (Berlin, Springer, 1932; vol. I: Philosophische

Weltorientierung; vol. II: Existenzerhellung; vol. III: Metaphysik).

THIRD LECTURE

1) E. Baumgarten has shown this in an interesting study on Franklin ("Benjamin Franklin und die Psychologie des amerikanischen Alltags," in *Neue Jahrbücher für Wissenschaft und Jugendbildung*, February, 1933, pp. 251 ff.). He shows how Franklin had developed principles for this type of communication which always went beyond merely factual communication. The sensitiveness of men in their stubbornness and hidden interests requires from anyone who thinks he possesses the truth with certitude and knows what is now right an urbane attitude, a willingness of both to listen to the other and to question seriously what one has oneself thought out and planned. All direct communications of the truth, instead of a questioning of it, destroy communication; the other does not really listen since he is no longer even questioned. Therefore the principles for communicating the truth are not less important than the communicated truth itself. Genuine and effective respect does not mean that we both remain unchanged in our opinions; perhaps later the opinion of the other will be more adapted to change mine. Cooperation demands, further, that one come to understand the defects of the matter. To wish to set up something finished and completed is to misunderstand the potentialities which lie in the concrete and, instead of perfection, ends in confusion. Only by granting room for free play can there be any union and, consequently, any perception of how the concrete matter is to be changed. So, it can even be required that we pass ourselves by, suspend all our opinions, in order to make an action possible which for the moment seems necessary.

2) Cf. my *Philosophie*, vol. II, pp. 50-117, on "Kommunication."

3) Cf. my *Philosophie*, vol. III, pp. 102-116, on "Das Gesetz des Tages und die Leidenschaft zur Nacht."

FIFTH LECTURE

1) The name is misleading if it appears to be restrictive. Philosophy can never wish to be anything but simple, ancient, eternal philosophy.

2) If we think about the perversions resulting from specious knowledge, which were explained in the last chapter—about the submersion of Existenz by its self-transformation into something knowable, by planned techniques for producing that out of which, as a fundamental source, one can will but which is destroyed when directly willed—then precisely this awareness of the possibilities lying in the nature of human thought has the consequence that true philosophy can not be the result of a plan like some means to an end. Knowledge of this error can protect one to a certain degree from deceptions, but can not enable one deliberately to work out anything positive. On the grounds of the infinite possibilities which have become visible, philosophizing is, more than ever before, an "experiment," that is, an act which goes beyond all rational purposes, beyond every goal. Out of answers from what I encounter, from what I myself risk in thought, emerges in new questions an awareness of something never ultimately there before me, but nevertheless existentially present to me as authentic Being. The criteria of truth lie in these existential standards, not merely in logical mechanisms.

Such reflections limit the significance of our sketch of contemporary philosophizing to mere pointers.

3) The philosophizing of Kant is supported by a trust in reason. The presupposition and end of his thinking is that reason in itself can not destroy, that contradictions can exist neither in thought nor in being. His long concern over the antinomies, those apparently irresolvable contradictions which emerge in thinking about the world, led him toward insight into the origins of reason out of which such illusion must necessarily come. And there he found consolation and courage for reason: "For what can you depend upon otherwise, if that which alone is called upon to dispose of all error, itself were corrupt and without hope of attaining peace and stable possessions?"

But Kant's reason had a large scope. It included, not only the understanding, but also the faculty of Ideas by which no object was cognized, and also the perception of the beautiful. This perception Kant explained as rationality in the mutual interplay of the cognitive faculties, imagination and the understanding, and of freedom and law. Without cognition of an object and without accomplishment of an act, this perception of the beautiful permitted the whole nature of man in its total rationality to become aware of both itself and of the supersensible substratum, but only in play.

And also, this wider conception of reason enabled Kant to go to the limits, where reason can no longer grasp; he was aware of the "secret," the "riddle," the "abyss." In particular, reason can not grasp how freedom is possible, that is, how the "revolution in mode of thought" can occur by which I can become positively free from the radical evil of my intelligible nature. "Grace" is something for him which reason does not oppose, but also something which reason can not "think in its maxims, nor take into consideration in its actions" without falling into fanaticism and the weakening of one's own moral responsibilities.

"Reason figures this way: if there is something more in the inexplorable region of the supernatural than it can comprehend, then that too unknown to it would work to the advantage of the good will."

Kant thus had a consciousness of the limits of reason which was transparent to itself and rested upon itself, and in such a way that what he was negatively aware of on these limits was expressed in its decisive depths in his consciousness of God.

But the idealism of Fichte, Schelling, and Hegel dropped out at the beginning all the limits to reason which Kant had seen, and finally, in Hegel, built a tower of Babel where everything was absorbed into a reason which now had a sense far beyond that of Kant. This reason is "mysticism for the understanding"; in its movement it absorbed the understanding without which it could not take a step, but its philosophizing wanted to be the absolute knowledge of an evolving rationality of all Being, the unity of the rational and the irrational. Such a reason recognized its limits now only in the indifferent, in bad infinity, in the impotence of nature to obey the concept, and as chance which was without essence.

This most consistent idealism, which reconciles everything with everything else, was already broken through by Fichte when later he regarded all empirical existence and the self-hood which suffuses it (i.e., that which becomes clear to reason) as a mere image of divinity and when he restored the irrational hiatus between freedom and God, between empirical existence and Being.

Schelling broke through idealism, which he retained however as his presupposition of a deductive presentation of pure rationality and which he called negative philosophy (since the path of this rational philosophy really is the perpetual subversion of every form of reason). He sketched out a positive philosophy by which he wanted to penetrate to the ground of all things, a ground however which was factual, not rational. This ground is historical and is to be understood as an event, but not grasped as a necessity. We can not go beyond it: "No one can lay any other basis than that which was laid at the beginning."

Schelling and Fichte both sought factual Being in the ground of all rationality, but, true as their axioms were, they never reached it either because they remained caught in the chains of their own idealism, or because they lacked the possible fulfillment of genuine experience.

4). In my published work, *Philosophie*, I intended to make a systematic study of the act of transcending: in philosophical world-orientation in order to loosen any possible enchainment to known things in the world; in the clarification of Existenz in order to recall and awaken to what man himself really is; in metaphysics in order to experience final limits and give intimations of Transcendence. The inner attitude of seeking communication in this philosophy is one which has abandoned with Kant the old objective metaphysics and, with Kierkegaard and Nietzsche, any repose in the totality of developed Spirit. It rejects that psychology which thinks it can exhaustively comprehend man as a whole, as well as every other form of the absolutization of scientific knowledge, which can only claim validity in factual investigations and for individual cases, in order to teach one to pass resolutely beyond these methodically limited ways of knowing. It is rooted in the original desire to know. For it alone can scientific knowledge of finite things in a broken world be clearly worked out without alteration of that knowledge (as I see it done in the investigations and accomplishment of Max Weber); for this philosophy alone is there any decisive separation between the cognition of finite things in experienceable existence and thinking in life through freedom and reason (as I see it in Kant). A thinking unfolds itself which is not merely a knowledge about something else to which it is related as to something alien, but a knowing which is an inner act, illuminating, awakening, or working its transformation.

The relation of such a philosophy to philosophical logic is this: what is rationally done in philosophy is, in philosophical logic, brought to methodical and formal awareness, along with all other modes of rationality.

5) One might wonder about "reflection" and "self-reflection," whose unlimited intensification was one of the accomplishments of Kierkegaard and Nietzsche which led to our new situation.

Reflection is nothing but those movements of thought which occur in the Encompassing of consciousness as such and in spirit, in forms which a methodology of a philosophical logic would handle. Infinite reflection arises through an unlimited impulse of reason in a human risk without reservation, an impulse which can stop itself only by hitting upon the Existenz which is supporting reason itself.

Self-reflection means three things. As psychological introspection, it establishes and interpets facts which now are whatever they are. As the clarification of Existenz, it sketches out possibilities for a multiplicity of meanings which let everything thought of assume other meanings, a clarification through which the freedom of inner activity of a substantial selfhood standing before its Transcendence should be awakened. As the self-consciousness of reason, it is a universal and comprehensive possibility for clarity about the modes of Being which exist for me, and about the modes of myself. It finds its explicit development in philosophical logic, which in origin and goal is philosophy itself.

Self-reflection as a distinctive fact is the object and source of psychology. As a medium for the selfhood of Existenz, it is itself the concrete philosophizing which illuminates Existenz, an inner deed. As the Encompassing of reason which is conscious of itself, it is actualized as logical self-consciousness.

In order to bring these relations into the greatest possible clarity, the basic problem must be posed and developed as to what thinking itself is and what the concept is. This goes beyond the scope of these lectures. But such a development would probably hold that the presupposition that thought and concepts are self-evident is incorrect; here we have a true abyss and, for philosophical logic, a decisive beginning for developing the origin of all possibilities of thought. Here we must ascend to a level quite alien to ordinary modes of thought, similiar yet also wholly different from that by which we have tried to apprehend the "Encompassing" in these lectures.

6) Cf. my *Philosophie*, vol. I, pp. 292 ff., for the relations of philosophy to religion, science, and art.

NOONDAY PAPERBACKS

EPITAPH OF A SMALL WINNER *Machado de Assis*	N101
AESTHETIC *Benedetto Croce*	N102
THE REVOLUTION IN PHYSICS *Louis de Broglie*	N103
PAN (a novel) *Knut Hamsun*	N104
LAOCOON *Gotthold Ephraim Lessing*	N105
A READER'S GUIDE TO T. S. ELIOT *George Williamson*	N106
A STUDY IN DOSTOEVSKY *Vyacheslav Ivanov*	N107
THE DANCE OF SHIVA *Ananda K. Coomaraswamy*	N108
THE JOURNEY TO THE EAST (a novel) *Hermann Hesse*	N109
NOA NOA: A Journal of the South Seas *Paul Gauguin*	N110
THE IMPOSTOR (a novel) *Jean Cocteau*	N111
LIVES OF THE ARTISTS *Giorgio Vasari*	N112
THE SUPREME IDENTITY *Alan W. Watts*	N113
THE TRANSCENDENCE OF THE EGO *Jean-Paul Sartre*	N114
GIMPEL THE FOOL and other stories *Isaac Bashevis Singer*	N115
THE STRUCTURE OF MUSIC: A Listener's Guide *Robert Erickson*	N116
REASON AND EXISTENZ *Karl Jaspers*	N117
AFTER THE LOST GENERATION *John W. Aldridge*	N118
YOUNG TORLESS (a novel) *Robert Musil*	N119
THE CHANGING FORMS OF ART *Patrick Heron*	N120
THE GREAT FAIR: Scenes from my Childhood *Sholom Aleichem*	N121
DOUBLE LIVES: An Autobiography *William Plomer*	N122
THE VERBAL ICON *W. K. Wimsatt*	N123
RELIGIOUS ART: From the 12th to the 18th Century *Emil Mâle*	N124
THE UNKNOWN CHEKHOV edited by *Avrahm Yarmolinsky*	N125
MYTH AND CHRISTIANITY *Karl Jaspers* and *Rudolf Bultmann*	N126
THE DONNE TRADITION *George Williamson*	N127
FATHERS AND SONS (a novel) *Ivan Turgenev;* tr. by GEORGE REAVEY	N128
MAN AND HIS BECOMING ACCORDING TO THE VEDANTA *René Guénon*	N129
ELPENOR (a novel) *Jean Giraudoux*	N130
MEMOIRS OF AN EGOTIST *Stendhal*	N131
CEZANNE *Roger Fry*	N132
THE GREEN CHAPEL (verse) *Barbara Gibbs*	N133
SATAN IN GORAY (a novel) *Isaac Bashevis Singer*	N134
NOONDAY 1 (stories, articles, poetry—including "The Last Summer" by Boris Pasternak) edited by *Cecil Hemley*	N135
A SHORT HISTORY OF PSYCHOTHERAPY *Nigel Walker*	N136
GREAT STORIES BY NOBEL PRIZE WINNERS edited by *Leo Hamalian* and *Edmond L. Volpe*	N137
A READER'S GUIDE TO WILLIAM BUTLER YEATS *John Unterecker*	N138
LECTURES ON THE FRENCH REVOLUTION *Lord Acton*	N139
NOONDAY 2 (stories, articles, poetry—including "Manhunt" by Alejo Carpentier) edited by *Cecil Hemley* and *Dwight W. Webb*	N140
THE INMOST LEAF (essays) *Alfred Kazin*	N141
THE FINANCIAL EXPERT (a novel) *R. K. Narayan*	N142
FROM CALIGARI TO HITLER: A Psychological History of the German Film *Siegfried Kracauer*	N143
STENDHAL: NOTES ON A NOVELIST *Robert M. Adams*	N144
AMONG WOMEN ONLY (a novel) *Cesare Pavese*	N145
COLLECTED POEMS *Louise Bogan*	N146
A READER'S GUIDE TO JAMES JOYCE *William York Tindall*	N147
A READER'S GUIDE TO GREAT TWENTIETH-CENTURY ENGLISH NOVELS *Frederick R. Karl* and *Marvin Magalaner*	N148
INTRODUCTION TO THE ART OF THE MOVIES edited by *Lewis Jacobs*	N149
NOONDAY 3 (stories, articles, poetry—including "Sunset" by Isaac Babel) edited by *Cecil Hemley* and *Dwight W. Webb*	N150
SURREALISM: THE ROAD TO THE ABSOLUTE *Anna Balakian*	N151
THE DEVIL IN THE HILLS (a novel) *Cesare Pavese*	N152
THE OTHER ALEXANDER (a novel) *Marguerite Liberaki*	N153
THE DILEMMA OF BEING MODERN (essays) *J. P. Hodin*	N154
RITUAL MAGIC *E. M. Butler*	N155
POEMS: A Selection *Leonie Adams*	N156